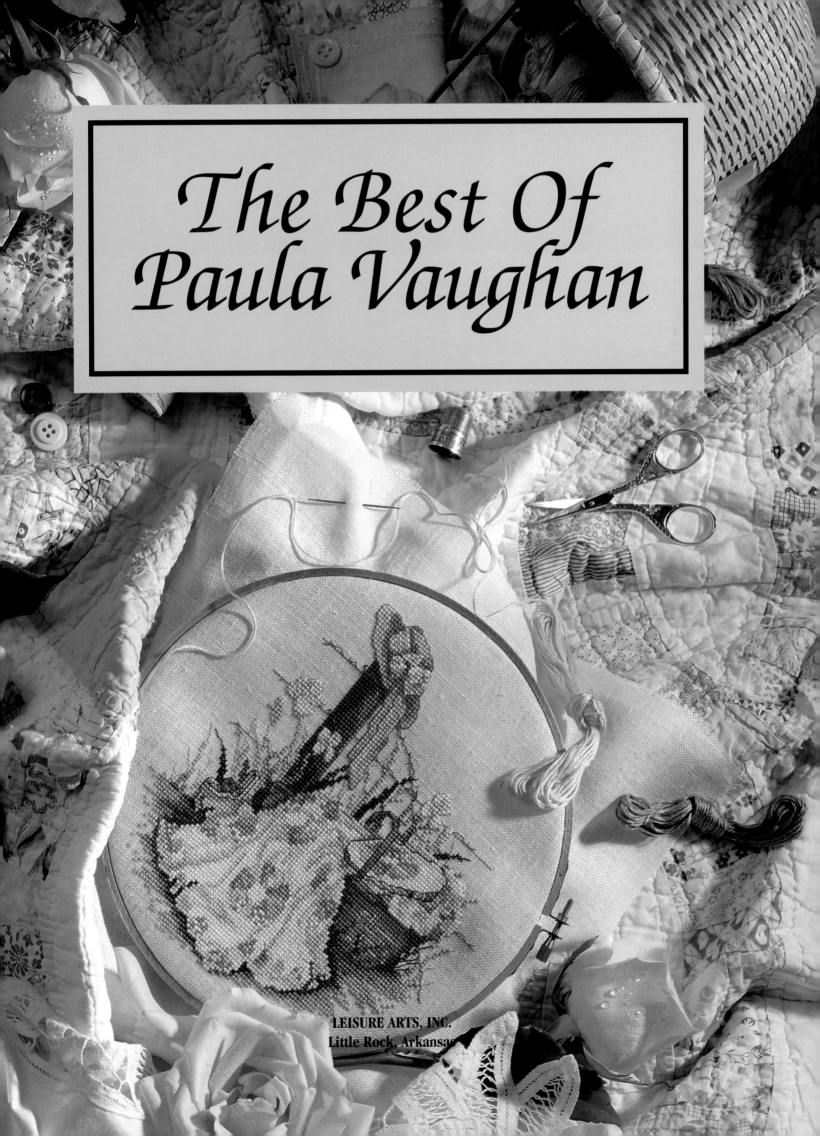

The Best Of
Paula Vaughan

LEISURE ARTS, INC.
Little Rock, Arkansas

EDITORIAL STAFF
Editor-in-Chief: Anne Van Wagner Childs
Executive Director: Sandra Graham Case
Executive Editor: Susan Frantz Wiles
Publications Director: Carla Bentley
Creative Art Director: Gloria Bearden
Production Art Director: Melinda Stout

PRODUCTION
Managing Editor: Teal Lee Elliott
Senior Editor: Laura Siar Holyfield
Technical Writers: Linda Bassett, Carolyn Breeding,
  Sandra White Buie, Renée M. DeLay, Donna Brown
  Hill, Karen Jackson, Tracy D. Thomas, and
  Pamela Fuller Young

EDITORIAL
Associate Editor: Linda L. Trimble
Senior Editorial Writer: Tammi Williamson Bradley
Editorial Writer: Terri Leming Davidson
Copy Editor: Laura Lee Weland

ART
Surface Stitchery Art Director: Andy Warren
Production Artists: Gabriel Wood, Susan Dailey,
  Deborah Kelly, and Steph Lindersmith
Photography Stylists: Karen Smart Hall,
  Christina Tiano, and Laura Bushmiaer

BUSINESS STAFF
Publisher: Steve Patterson
Controller: Tom Siebenmorgen
Retail Sales Director: Richard Tignor
Retail Marketing Director: Pam Stebbins
Retail Customer Services Director: Margaret Sweetin
Marketing Manager: Russ Barnett
Executive Director of Marketing and Circulation:
  Guy A. Crossley
Fulfillment Manager: Byron L. Taylor
Print Production Manager: Laura Lockhart
Print Production Coordinator: Nancy Reddick Lister

A special word of thanks goes to Linda Culp Calhoun and
Jane Chandler for their beautiful needlework adaptations.

Library of Congress Catalog Number 94-77913
International Standard Book Number 0-942237-49-8

Table of Contents

Introducing Paula Vaughan

*M*eeting Paula Vaughan, one is immediately drawn to her easygoing manner and endearing smile, which she shares generously. Her conversations are often sprinkled with laughter, and much like her paintings, Paula has a soft, decidedly feminine personality.

A beloved artist whose romantic images have captured the hearts of cross stitchers the world over, Paula says she knew very little about needlework only nine years ago. That's when Leisure Arts first contacted her with the idea of adapting her art to cross stitch. She admits she was apprehensive.

"I thought, 'They want to do what *with my paintings?'* I didn't have the faintest idea what cross stitch was."

However, her art publisher convinced her to give the new market a try. "Needless to say, it has been wonderful!" she says. "I was as proud of my first leaflet as I was my first limited print."

Since then, stitchers have enjoyed her beautiful designs in over 60 cross stitch leaflets, magazine features, and hardcover books published by Leisure Arts. In The Best of Paula Vaughan, we've gathered Paula's most popular cross stitch adaptations together in one volume.

Paula says one of the really wonderful things that's come out of her relationship with Leisure Arts is that she hears from women all across the country. Every once in a while, she'll receive a cross-stitched piece in the mail picturing one of her designs. "It almost breaks my heart when they send them, because they've spent all those hours stitching the pieces."

Pleased that her art appeals most to everyday people, Paula says her audience encompasses all ages. However, she points out a distinction between those who buy her prints and those who create her needlework designs.

"The collectors who buy the prints are very nice, and I really love them, but they're not as personally connected with me as the ladies who do counted cross stitch. The stitchers tell me that they feel like we do these projects together."

Paula says that at needlework shows, stitchers like to tell her which of her designs they finished first and which is their favorite. "It's very important to them. In fact, a lot of ladies will bring their framed stitched pieces to the shows for me to sign the mats."

No longer a stranger to this needlecraft, Paula recently tried her hand at stitching a project. "I bought some waste canvas when I was making a dress for my granddaughter, and I stitched her initials on the collar. You can't tell what the initials are," she says between chuckles. "Actually, they look like chicks, but I did it! So I'm no longer an inexperienced cross stitcher!"

Paula says stitching those three initials gave her an even greater respect for the crafters who create her designs. "I love crafts, but then after I started painting, it became such a passion that I gave up everything else."

Her introduction to painting can be credited to her sister-in-law, who believed Paula had to be artistic, since both of her brothers were talented artists. "I had never really done any painting," Paula explains.

"She [the sister-in-law] came over one day and we struggled through a piece. She knew I was hooked after that. It was so much fun! I still have some of those early paintings. You could finish one in an hour back then," she remembers. "You just took a pallet knife and globbed the paint on!"

For a while, Paula simply copied other people's designs, and painted on wood and furniture rather than canvas. "I guess one of the hardest things to do was to let go of other people's designs and do something creative on my own. I think that's the hardest step for every artist."

Reminiscing about those early experiences, Paula recalls a favorite anecdote. "My first easel was an old wooden highchair with an enamel tray that I used for both of my children. Mother bought it in 1942, during the war. It worked out really well because I could prop my painting against the back and use the tray to hold my paints." With laughter punctuating her story, Paula continues, "I had to really get that tray clean afterward, because my boys would have eaten the paint!"

Paula began her art career working with oils, and then after about seven years, she switched to watercolors using a dry-brush approach. "I tried the wet-on-wet technique, and that water started flowing all over the place!"

It took almost fourteen years for the self-taught artist to be "discovered" by the art community. "I never used to let anyone see my work," she says with characteristic humility. "I'd only give my paintings to Mother and Dad. Parents will hang anything!"

Luckily, Paula's parents weren't the only ones who appreciated her talent.

Early on, when she often threw away her watercolors, one of her neighbors retrieved several paintings from the trash and took them to be framed. Paula was quite surprised when the frame shop owners called and wanted to see more of her work. Reluctantly, she agreed.

"One day I decided to take about five paintings in, and they sold! I couldn't believe it," she says. Paula is still a little amazed at her success.

She continued to sell her original paintings through the shop until the demand became greater than she could supply. Then she ventured into publishing her art in limited-edition prints. After printing the first two designs on her own, Paula joined a publishing house.

"I knew right away that I didn't want to be in the marketing end of the business. In fact, the only way I sold the prints to anyone was if they were friends of mine, and they called. I just wouldn't get out and go to shows," she admits.

In those early years, Paula's "studio" was in her living room. "When the boys were little, they just knew to stay away from my things. It was confined to such a small area. But that may have been better, because now my studio is such a mess!" she says.

"By the time I get through painting, I have sketches everywhere, and I don't clean anything up while I'm painting. It's just a disaster area! Then, after I finish the painting, I'll clean everything up." Mischievously she adds, "Until I start the next painting!"

Today, her second-floor studio sits "way up in the trees" and has lots of big windows all across the back.

It's from this sunny haven that Paula re-creates images of a bygone era, when women fashioned colorful patchwork quilts and tended dooryard gardens full of flowers — quiet endeavors that many of us would enjoy today.

A perfectionist when it comes to her art, Paula says, "When you live with your work every day, you can become possessed by it, and when your studio is at home, you can't leave it. If something goes wrong, you're not going to sleep at night. You're going to go up there, and if it takes all night you're going to straighten the problem out."

Paula confesses that there are times when she'll paint for six weeks straight and, except for going to church on Sunday, that's all she does. "All depending on the time of year (and what the deadlines are!), I go into these working fits."

Surprisingly, Paula reveals that she has never been pleased with her paintings. "I think if you're ever pleased with your work, you need to quit painting," she says philosophically. "If I can get what's in my head onto the canvas, then I'll be happy. But somewhere between my head and the canvas, a lot of changes take place!"

Paula says she's uncomfortable viewing her work in galleries, and she doesn't like to hang her work at home. "I'll look at it and think, 'Why did I do this, or why didn't I do that?' There's always a part of a painting that you had so much trouble with, and when you look at the painting you never see the good, only the bad."

When she finishes a painting, Paula's mood turns melancholy. "I've found that if I can have another painting going in my mind, then I'm saved. But if I say, 'I'm taking two weeks off and going shopping and to lunch with my friends,' I'm so depressed."

Her solution? "I've learned to never let my mind be still or think, 'When I get through with this one ...'"

While her fans have described her style as "romantic" and "nostalgic realism," Paula believes that it's really quite varied. She says her recent oils most typify her style, and adds that whatever piece she worked on last is her favorite, because she develops a sentimental attachment to every painting.

Still adjusting to her incredible success, Paula thinks of herself as "a typical Southern woman. I'm more of a country person than a Victorian person when it comes to my personal things," she says. "I suppose you'd describe my tastes as soft country, or country Victorian."

Paula is also a talented seamstress, a skill for which she credits her mother and grandmothers. "Growing up, we didn't have a lot of money, but the ladies liked the nice things, so they made them." Paula says her mother sewed a new dress for her every week.

Inspired by their creativity, Paula says she'd like to try her hand at designing Victorian-style fashions. "I'd love to design children's clothes and wedding dresses. I want to design a full line of clothes."

For now, Paula's fashion designing is confined to the canvas, where she creates elaborate, authentically detailed Victorian ensembles.

Many of the dresses featured in her early designs were borrowed from friends or found in antique shops and flea markets. "Now I compose in my head and design the dresses as I paint," Paula explains.

An avid antique collector, Paula finds many of the props for her paintings in out-of-the-way shops. "Most of the time when I'm out antiquing, I'm looking for something for paintings. But I never go with anything particular in mind, since I collect a lot of things."

Indeed, she does! Paula's vast assortment of nostalgic collectibles includes quilts, china teapots, satin-bound books, a spinning wheel, and of course, a closetful of exquisite Victorian apparel.

Another subject that has made Paula such a popular artist is her beautiful florals. With a bit of pride, she says that many of the vibrant bouquets she paints are from her flower garden. She admits, however, that her husband is the real gardener in the family. "He always brings in flowers for me. And when there are pretty roses, he'll bring me a bouquet."

A nature lover, she especially enjoys the changing of the seasons to spring and fall. "After the hard winter, spring is wonderful!" she says excitedly. "When you see those first buds, and the daffodils and crocus come up, it's so beautiful. You walk down to the mailbox, and you see the little sprouts.

"And in the fall," she continues, "there's just a feeling in the air! You get up in the morning, and your soul just wants to burst! I hate exercise, but I'll even take a walk just to enjoy the beauty."

Paula's painting takes up much of her time — sometimes she works through the night — but she still manages to find time for herself.

To relax, Paula says she likes to grab a cup of coffee and sit in her porch swing. "I'm really not a hard person to please. I do love to shop, and right now baby clothes are my favorite thing to shop for," says the new grandmother.

Reading is another of Paula's hobbies, and she thoroughly enjoys a good mystery. "I read myself to sleep every night," she says, "I guess that's the only time my mind stops working on my paintings."

Paula takes all of her success one day at a time, though. "God has just blessed me so much, and once it's over, that's fine. It's just a special gift He's given me. This is something fun and great in life, and when it's over, it's over. But as long as He's with me and guides me, I feel like I'm in good shape whatever I do."

Cherished Moments

In this memento-filled scene, Paula proudly showcases an assortment of her personal treasures. A bouquet of the roses that grow wild near Paula's home is beautifully displayed in a porcelain pitcher from her collection. The wooden keepsake box was a graduation gift from a furniture store in her hometown, and the tiny locket in front of the box holds pictures of her grandparents. Tied with a satin ribbon, a stack of love letters lies atop one of Paula's favorite books, Anne of Green Gables.

Chart on pages 60-63

The Quilter

Incredibly beautiful and decidedly practical, quilts of yesteryear gave women an avenue for creating art with needle and thread. The second design in a series of paintings created in honor of needlewomen, "The Quilter" features a Grandmother's Fan quilt pieced from a kaleidoscope of colorful fabrics. On the original quilt, Paula says, the stitcher had embroidered the flowers in the corner of each quilt block.

Chart on pages 64-65

Tea, Roses and Romance

Paula's love of flowers is evident in this exquisitely detailed painting of fresh roses, sunny jonquils, and other delicate blooms. The pretty teapot in this romantic scene was the first piece in her collection of antique teapots, some of which she creatively displays on a bathroom shelf in her home — a charming and unexpected place to show off her collectibles.

Chart on pages 66-69

Let's Pretend

Delicately patterned wallpaper often helps to establish the mood in Paula's paintings. She says the first time she began a painting that included wallpaper, she went into the attic at her husband's grandmother's house to see what kind of paper was popular during the early part of the century. "It just so happened it was roses. What could be better for a Paula Vaughan painting!" Here, the artist chose a pretty design of peach roses to accentuate the feminine appeal of a lady's dressing room.

Chart on pages 70-71

15

Love Songs

A nostalgic keyboard like this melodeon was often a social centerpiece in the Victorian home. Filling the air with a lilting song, it set the stage for many delightful evenings, when budding musicians delighted guests with enchanting recitals. On such occasions, a love song was sure to be requested by a young suitor — and dedicated to a blushing miss.

Chart on pages 72-75

Quilting Lessons

In bygone days, instruction in needlework was a vital part of every young lady's training. Recalling her own early quilting lessons, Paula says, "When I was little, my grandmother sat me on the floor with all the quilt pieces and said, 'You can put these colors together any way you want.' It's just one of those fleeting moments that stick with you." These childhood memories inspired Paula to create this lovely piece as a gift for a dear friend.

Chart on pages 76-77

19

Aunt Verdi's Porch

A tribute to Paula's grandmother, Verdi, this tranquil design calls up warm and wonderful memories. "She would have appreciated the quiet of a porch like this one to sit and stitch," Paula says. The beautiful Crazy-Patch quilt draped across the rocker is a masterful arrangement of fancy patches edged with briar stitches. Paula fondly recalls that each piece of velvet on the quilt is embroidered with a flower.

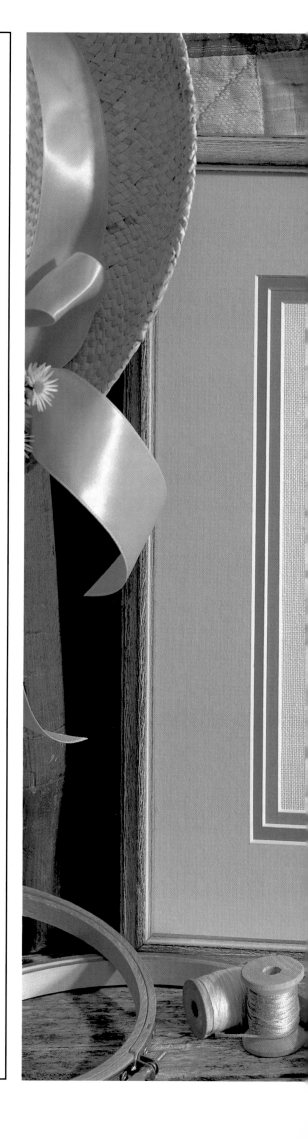

Chart on pages 78-79

21

A Cameo of the Past

The treasures found among a Victorian lady's accoutrements offer a wealth of inspiration for Paula's paintings. This wardrobe, filled with hatboxes, shoes, and gowns, is a family heirloom, but many of the old-fashioned items that she paints are purchased at flea markets and antique shops. Paula discovered the pink dress in this design in the attic of a Kentucky antique shop.

Chart on pages 80-81

23

Summer Breeze

Paula's paintings have a unique warmth and familiarity about them, perhaps because she incorporates images from her life into her work. For example, this exquisite Flower Basket quilt belonged to a friend, and the tree swing was inspired by memories of a favorite aunt. The woman returning from the garden is Paula's portrayal of her friend Mary.

Chart on pages 82-85

From This Day Forward

This sentimental wedding-day scene captures a bride's quiet, reflective moments just before the ceremony. As a touch of "something old" and "something borrowed," Paula used a friend's antique floral quilt as the model for the pretty rug. The canopied bed, "something new" handcrafted by Paula's husband as a wedding present for her, is covered with a Bridal Wreath quilt. "Something blue" is the cloudless sky — what bride could ask for a more beautiful day!

Chart on pages 86-89

Spring Remembered

Paula painted this airy springtime scene after visiting Williamsburg, Virginia, where she fell in love with picket fences. Here, the quaint fencing, edged with a profusion of climbing roses and lovely irises, has enticed a needlewoman outdoors to enjoy the fresh sunshine. Perhaps our quilter has just stepped away from her work to chat with a passing friend.

Chart on pages 90-91

Sunlight and Silhouettes

Romantic French doors swing wide to welcome the warm afternoon light bathing this wistful scene, which includes several of Paula's beloved collectibles. Draped across her grandmother's wicker rocker are a dainty antique camisole, a petticoat, and a pair of pantalets. Silhouettes, such as the two displayed on the wall, are of special interest to Paula. She says portraits of this type are rare today, and hers, from 1934, are inscribed, "For your wedding shower."

Chart on pages 92-95

Victorian Bouquet

Vibrant bouquets are favorite subjects for Paula to paint. This arrangement, displayed in an enamelware pitcher, reflects her special affection for colorful blossoms. She readily admits, however, that her husband is the gardener in the family. "He always brings in flowers for me," she says with a smile, "especially when there are pretty roses. It's so nice to come down and see beautiful, fresh flowers after I've been up in the studio all day."

Chart on pages 96-97

Sisters Three

Like many of Paula's paintings, this genteel reflection inspires us to recall the pastimes of a more graceful period. One can easily imagine three charming sisters dressed in these lovely frocks and flower-strewn chapeaus. Such ensembles would have been high fashion for a Sunday afternoon stroll in the park, or perhaps an enchanting soiree.

Chart on pages 98-99

The Fabric Of Dreams

In olden days, keepsake quilts were often pieced from prized fabrics that had been carefully saved over the years. Each bit of material represented a person, event, or story that the quilter could enjoy recalling as time passed. Double Wedding Ring quilts, in particular, were frequently crafted with such sentimental scraps. The lovely comforter shown here is reminiscent of the one Paula's grandmother made for her as a wedding present. It was pieced using fabric scraps from Paula's old skirts.

Chart on pages 100-101

Something Old, Something New

Paula paints one wedding picture each year, and she says they're always well-received because of their sentimental appeal. She captures that nostalgic feeling beautifully in this heart-touching scene, which celebrates the beloved wedding day tradition of wearing something old and something new. The heirlooms portrayed here — a rose-trimmed bridal gown and veil, a Double Wedding Ring quilt, and a china tea service — are sure to be cherished by the bride and passed along someday to her own daughter.

Chart on pages 102-105

Yesterday's Dream

Draped across a cedar chest, this Flower Garden quilt is one of several cozy comforters being put away after a long winter. Paula says the fabrics in the original patchwork are from the Civil War period. An antiques buff, she enjoys featuring old-fashioned items in her paintings, like this spinning wheel and nostalgic pitcher and bowl.

Chart on pages 106-107

Reflections of the Past

Set against a backdrop of delicate floral wallpaper, this design showcases a lovely dress such as a Victorian lady might have worn. Its reflection in the old-fashioned dressing mirror reveals a spray of flowers pinned at the neckline. Early in her career, Paula borrowed antique dresses to study while she painted. "Now, I design them as I go along," she says.

Chart on pages 108-109

Rose of Sharon

Having grown up with broad, airy porches to play on, Paula finds these cozy havens a favorite subject to paint. She remembers her grandmother's spacious veranda as a hub of family activity, where folks often gathered to enjoy each other's company and catch a passing breeze. The lovely Rose of Sharon quilt shown here captures the fresh, outdoor feeling of summer in the country.

Chart on pages 110-113

The Upstairs Sewing Room

An accomplished seamstress herself, Paula features her grandmother's old treadle sewing machine in this charming scene. The pretty matching dresses for mother and daughter hold a special appeal for Paula. "I always dreamed of having a little girl," she says, "and I thought how nice it would be to dress alike. Since I didn't have a daughter, I put a little girl's dress in this design."

Chart on pages 114-115

Summers Remembered

Pink Ribbon

This charming design was the first of Paula's watercolors to be charted for cross stitch. "The adaptations of all my paintings have been beautiful," the artist says, "but for some reason, when I see this one stitched, I think it's one of the very best." In this idyllic scene, a Dresden Plate quilt from Paula's private collection is beautifully displayed spilling from a quilter's basket.

Chart on page 116

49

A Little
Girl's Fancy

In this sweet design, we take a peek into a little girl's fanciful world of make-believe. Her admirable collection of playthings includes a Sweet Sue doll (sitting in the rocking chair) that Paula received when she was eight years old. "You didn't get a lot of dolls back then," she recalls. "You had one doll, then your mother made new clothes for it every Christmas after that." Paula still has the doll and its clothes, and she admits that over the years, "I have taken them out and played with them by myself." But she adds gleefully, "Now, I can't wait for my granddaughter to get old enough to play with me!"

Chart on pages 118-121

A Bouquet for Elizabeth

This romantic scene was inspired by a prettily bound edition of Flowers, *a compilation of writings by Paula's favorite poet, Robert Browning. The vibrant piece, named for the poet's wife, Elizabeth, showcases a proliferation of fresh cuttings in a wicker basket. A bonnet and book of verse lying nearby suggest that the gardener has spent a pleasant day in her garden counting the ways to love.*

Chart on pages 122-123

53

The Seamstress

Paula's admiration for needlewomen inspired her to create this design celebrating the exquisite creations of the seamstress. The old-fashioned sewing machine here is similar to the one on which Paula learned to sew. Thinking back, she recalls how her mother kept her in the latest fashions. "We would go to town and look at the dresses in the windows, then go home, and Mother would duplicate them," Paula says proudly.

Chart on pages 124-125

Wedding Ring Bouquet

A traditional Double Wedding Ring quilt is the focus of this sentimental vignette, which combines two of Paula's favorite themes — fresh flowers and old-fashioned quilts. She says this popular patchwork pattern is one of her favorites to paint because women relate to it so well. "I try to incorporate quilts that people are familiar with and feel comfortable with," Paula says.

Chart on pages 126-127

Summers Remembered

Blue Bonnet

An enthusiastic quilt collector, Paula was greatly influenced in her love for this art form by her grandmothers, both of whom were devoted quilters "out of necessity." She pays tribute to their special bond with this relaxing scene, which includes her grandmother's ladder-back chair and blue bonnet. A pretty Grandmother's Fan quilt adds to the nostalgia.

Chart on page 117

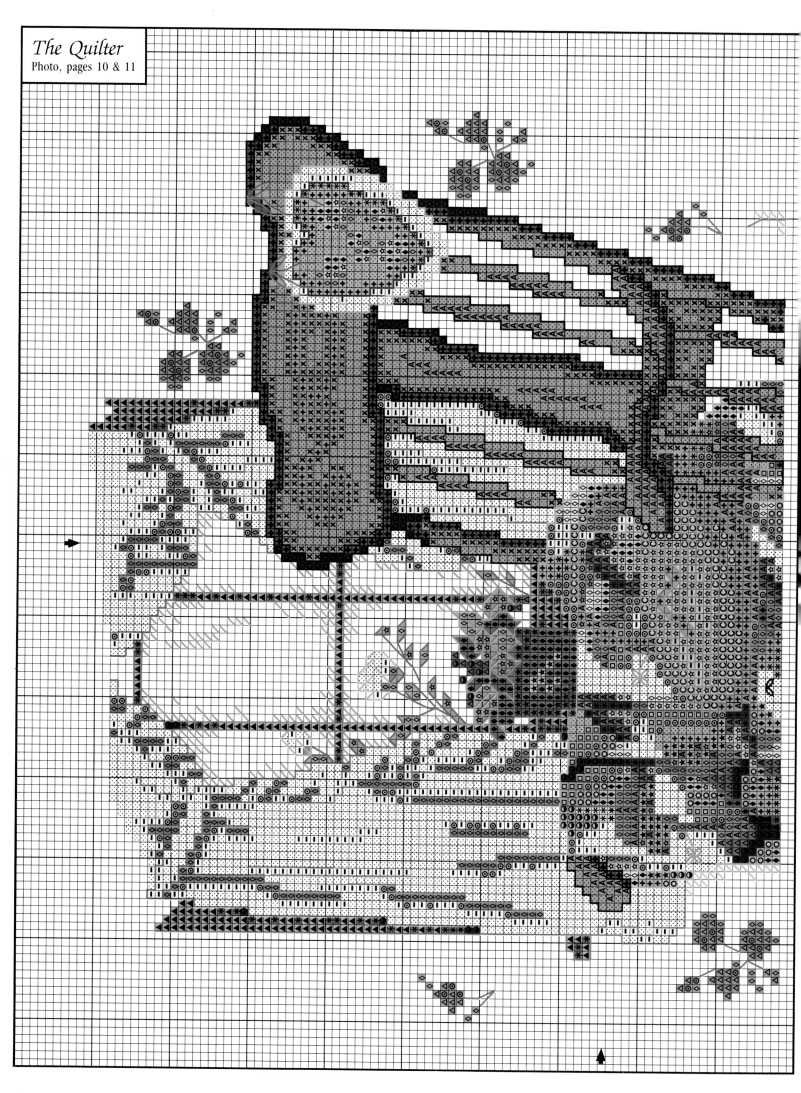

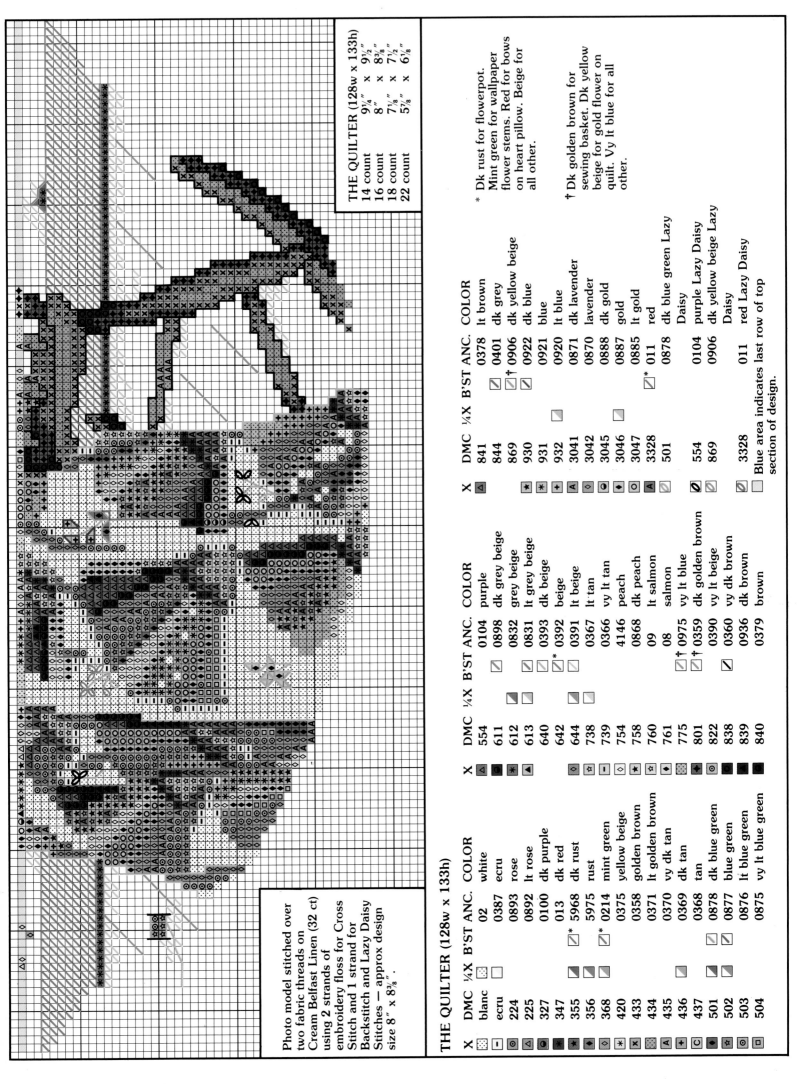

Photo model stitched over two fabric threads on Cream Belfast Linen (32 ct) using 2 strands of embroidery floss for Cross Stitch and 1 strand for Backstitch and Lazy Daisy Stitches — approx design size 8" x 8⅜".

THE QUILTER (128w x 133h)

	14 count	9¼" x 9½"
	16 count	8" x 8⅜"
	18 count	7⅛" x 7½"
	22 count	5⅞" x 6⅛"

* Dk rust for flowerpot. Mint green for wallpaper flower stems. Red for bows on heart pillow. Beige for all other.

† Dk golden brown for sewing basket. Dk yellow beige for gold flower on quilt. Vy lt blue for all other.

THE QUILTER (128w x 133h)

X	DMC	¼X	B'ST	ANC.	COLOR
	blanc			02	white
	ecru			0387	ecru
	224			0893	rose
	225			0892	lt rose
	327			0100	dk purple
	347			013	dk red
	355		*	5968	dk rust
	356			5975	rust
	368		*	0214	mint green
	420			0375	yellow beige
	433			0358	golden brown
	434			0371	lt golden brown
	435			0370	vy dk tan
	436			0369	dk tan
	437			0368	tan
	501			0878	dk blue green
	502			0877	blue green
	503			0876	lt blue green
	504			0875	vy lt blue green

X	DMC	¼X	B'ST	ANC.	COLOR
	554			0104	purple
	611			0898	dk grey beige
	612			0832	grey beige
	613			0831	lt grey beige
	640			0393	dk beige
	642		*	0392	beige
	644			0391	lt beige
	738			0367	lt tan
	739			0366	vy lt tan
	754			4146	peach
	758			0868	dk peach
	760			09	lt salmon
	761			08	salmon
	775		†	0975	vy lt blue
	801		†	0359	dk golden brown
	822			0390	vy lt beige
	838			0360	vy dk brown
	839			0936	dk brown
	840			0379	brown

X	DMC	¼X	B'ST	ANC.	COLOR
	841			0378	lt brown
	844			0401	dk grey
	869		†	0906	dk yellow beige
	930			0922	dk blue
	931			0921	blue
	932			0920	lt blue
	3041			0871	dk lavender
	3042			0870	lavender
	3045			0888	dk gold
	3046			0887	gold
	3047			0885	lt gold
	3328		*	011	red
	501			0878	dk blue green Lazy Daisy
	554			0104	purple Lazy Daisy
	869			0906	dk yellow beige Lazy Daisy
	3328			011	red Lazy Daisy

Blue area indicates last row of top section of design.

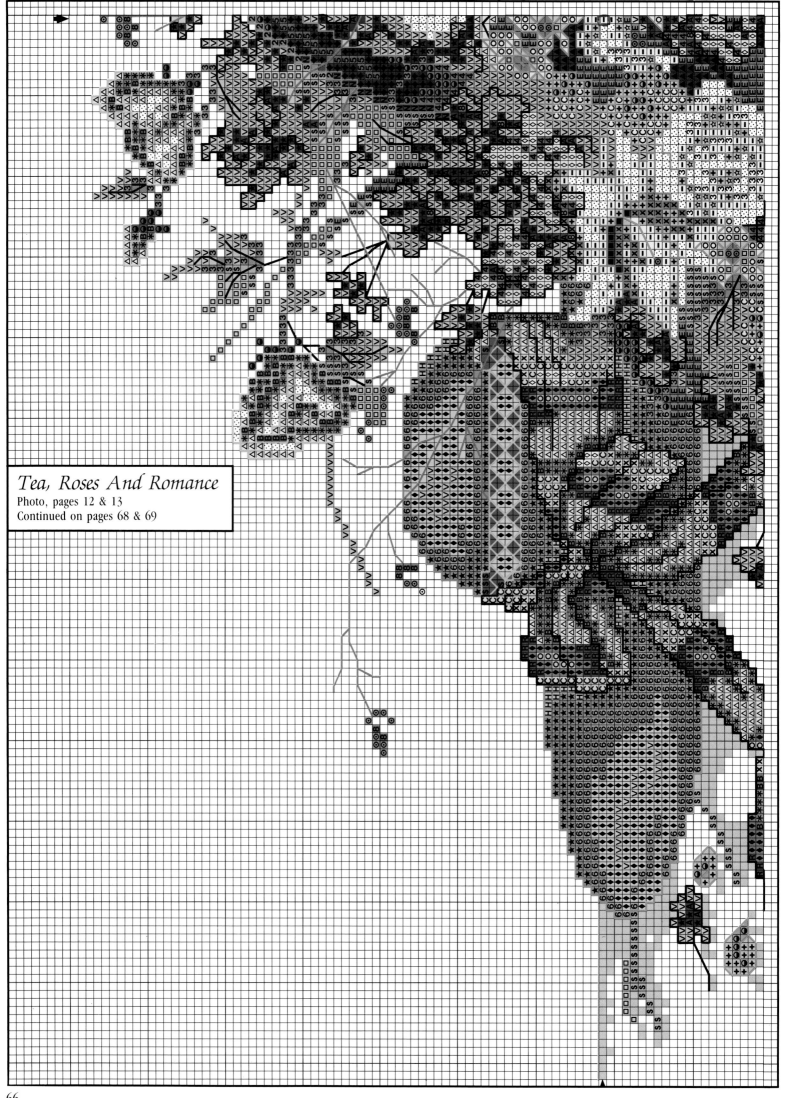

Tea, Roses And Romance
Photo, pages 12 & 13
Continued on pages 68 & 69

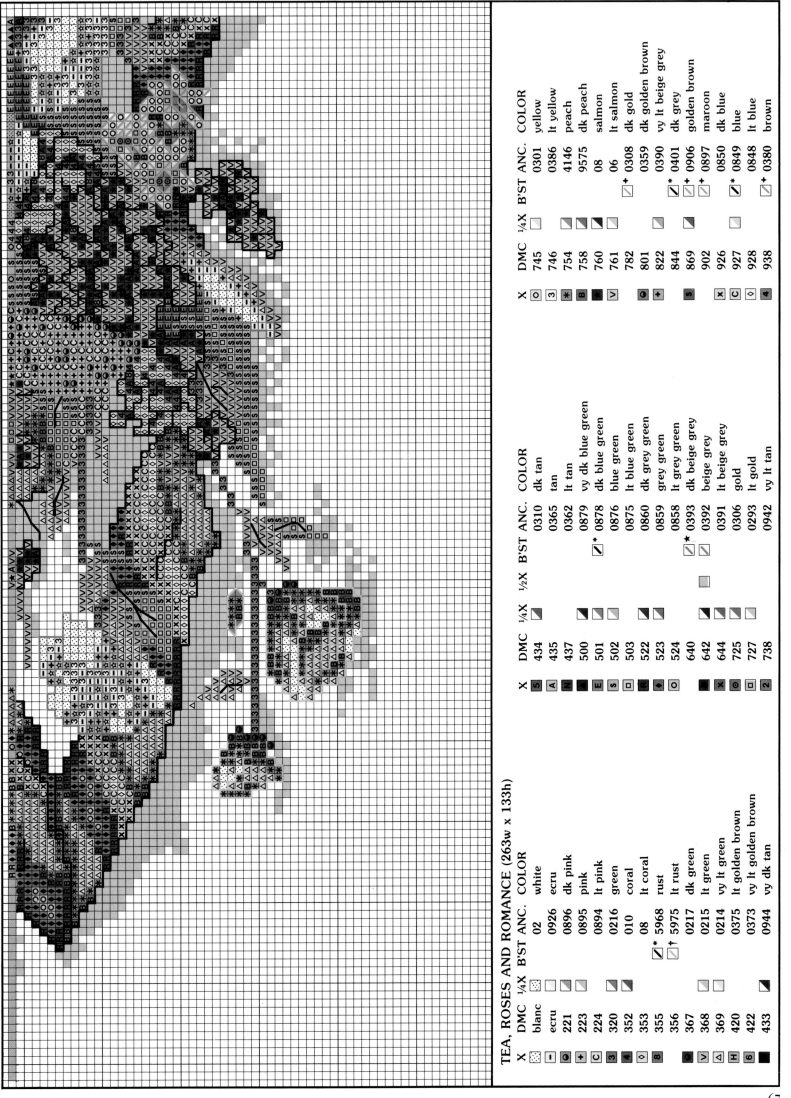

TEA, ROSES AND ROMANCE (263w x 133h)

X	DMC	¼X	B'ST	ANC.	COLOR
	blanc			02	white
–	ecru			0926	ecru
◑	221			0896	dk pink
+	223			0895	pink
C	224			0894	lt pink
3	320			0216	green
◀	352			010	coral
◈	353			08	lt coral
8	355		▨*	5968	rust
	356		▨†	5975	lt rust
◐	367			0217	dk green
▽	368			0215	lt green
△	369			0214	vy lt green
H	420			0375	lt golden brown
6	422			0373	vy lt golden brown
■	433		◣	0944	vy dk tan

X	DMC	¼X	½X	B'ST	ANC.	COLOR
5	434	◥			0310	dk tan
A	435				0365	tan
N	437				0362	lt tan
◧	500	◥			0879	vy dk blue green
E	501			◣*	0878	dk blue green
s	502	◥			0876	blue green
□	503				0875	lt blue green
R	522				0860	dk grey green
◆	523	◥			0859	grey green
◯	524				0858	lt grey green
■	640			◣★	0393	dk beige grey
X	642		▨		0392	beige grey
◉	644				0391	lt beige grey
◎	725				0306	gold
◻	727				0293	lt gold
2	738				0942	vy lt tan

X	DMC	¼X	B'ST	ANC.	COLOR
◯	745			0301	yellow
3	746			0386	lt yellow
✳	754			4146	peach
B	758			9575	dk peach
✚	760			08	salmon
V	761			06	lt salmon
	782	◺	+	0308	dk gold
◐	801			0359	dk golden brown
+	822			0390	vy lt beige grey
s	844	◣	+	0401	dk grey
◉	869	◺	+	0906	golden brown
×	902			0897	maroon
C	926			0850	dk blue
◇	927	◣	*	0849	blue
◪	928			0848	lt blue
◣	938	◺	+	0380	brown

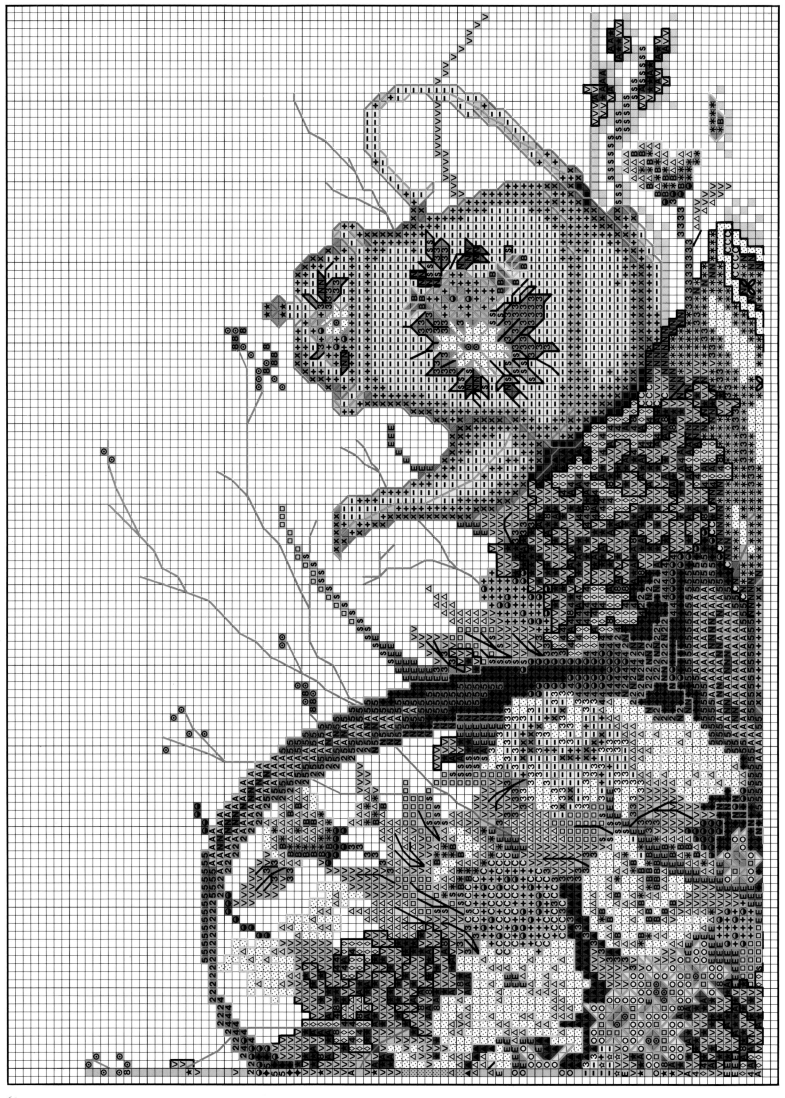

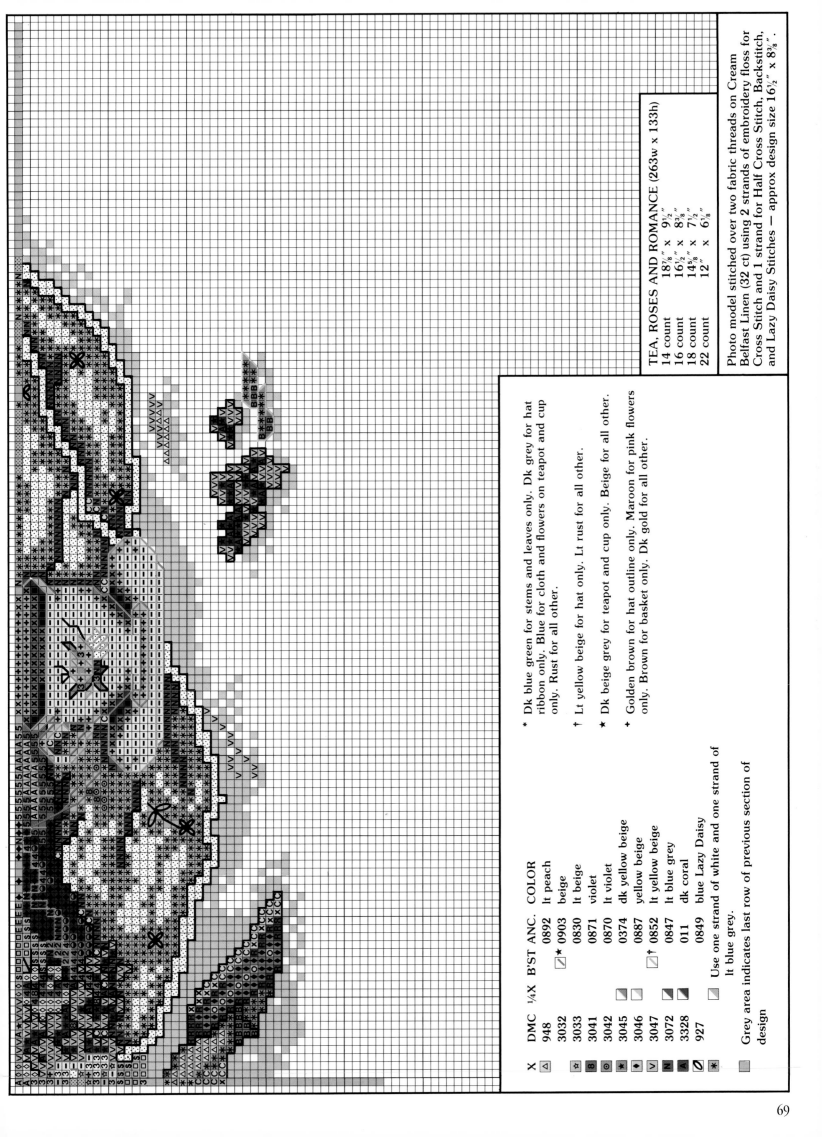

TEA, ROSES AND ROMANCE (263w x 133h)

14 count	18⅞" x	9½"
16 count	16½" x	8⅜"
18 count	14⅝" x	7½"
22 count	12" x	6⅛"

Photo model stitched over two fabric threads on Cream Belfast Linen (32 ct) using 2 strands of embroidery floss for Cross Stitch and 1 strand for Half Cross Stitch, Backstitch, and Lazy Daisy Stitches — approx design size 16½" x 8⅜".

* Dk blue green for stems and leaves only. Dk grey for hat ribbon only. Blue for cloth and flowers on teapot and cup only. Rust for all other.

† Lt yellow beige for hat only. Lt rust for all other.

★ Dk beige grey for teapot and cup only. Beige for all other.

+ Golden brown for hat outline only. Maroon for pink flowers only. Brown for basket only. Dk gold for all other.

X	¼X	B'ST	ANC.	COLOR
			DMC	
	△		948	0892	lt peach
		★	3032	0903	beige
✦	✦		3033	0830	lt beige
B			3041	0871	violet
⊙			3042	0870	lt violet
★			3045	0374	dk yellow beige
◆			3046	0887	yellow beige
V		†| 3047	0852	lt yellow beige
N			3072	0847	lt blue grey
A			3328	011	dk coral
∅			927	0849	blue Lazy Daisy
✱					Use one strand of white and one strand of lt blue grey.
▨					Grey area indicates last row of previous section of design

69

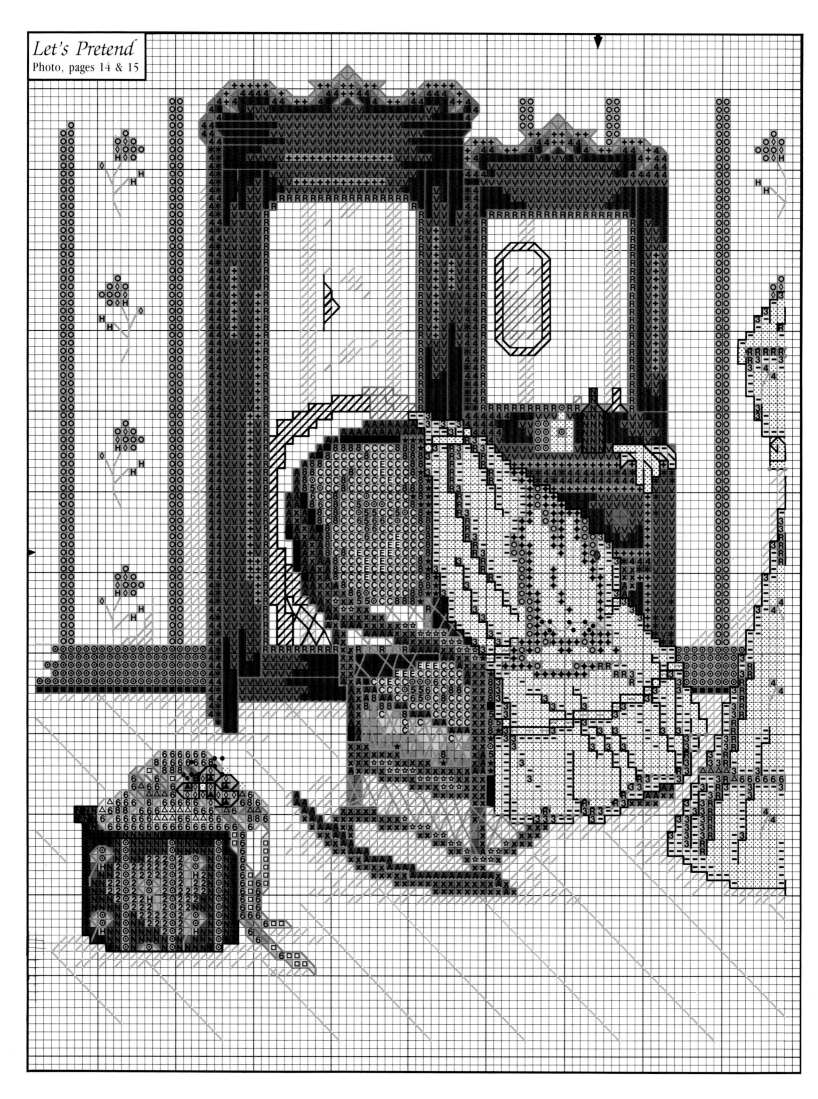

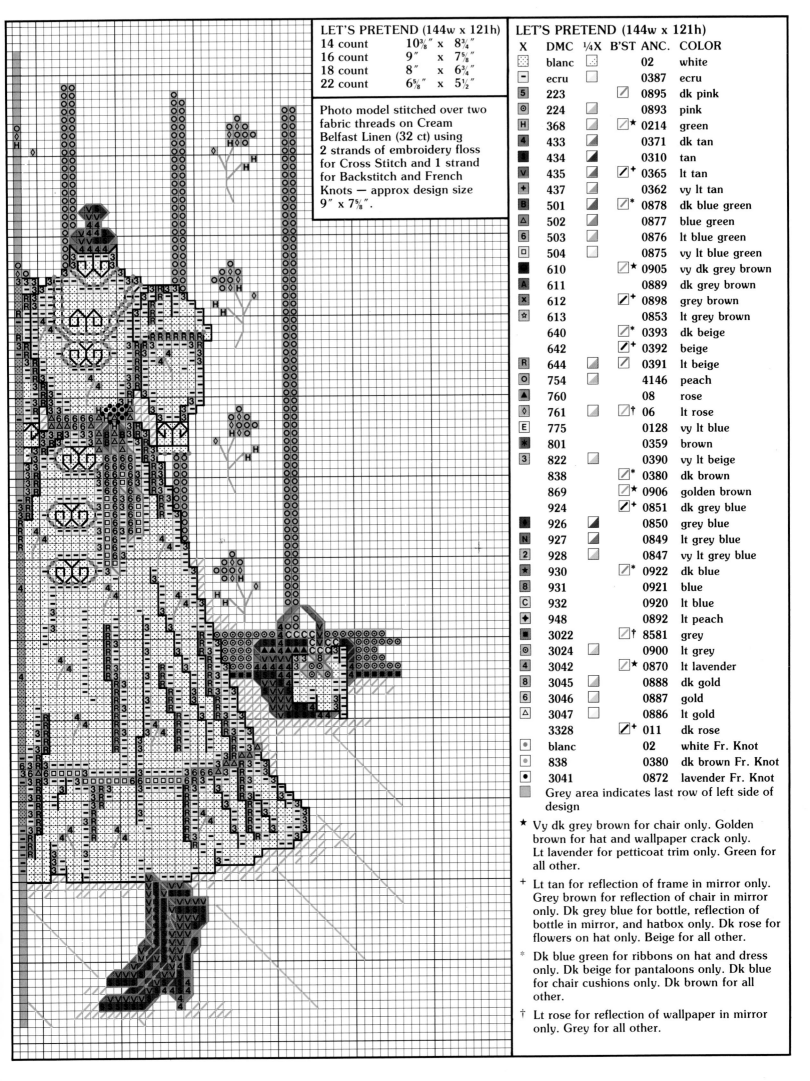

X	DMC	¼X	B'ST	ANC.	COLOR
⌗	blanc	⌗		02	white
−	ecru	□		0387	ecru
5	223		◹	0895	dk pink
⊙	224		◹	0893	pink
H	368	□	◹★	0214	green
4	433		◹	0371	dk tan
◼	434		◣	0310	tan
V	435		◹+	0365	lt tan
+	437		◹	0362	vy lt tan
B	501		◹★	0878	dk blue green
△	502		◹	0877	blue green
6	503		◹	0876	lt blue green
⊡	504		□	0875	vy lt blue green
◼	610		◹	0905	vy dk grey brown
A	611			0889	dk grey brown
X	612		◹+	0898	grey brown
☆	613			0853	lt grey brown
	640		◹★	0393	dk beige
	642		◹+	0392	beige
R	644	◹	◹	0391	lt beige
⊙	754			4146	peach
▲	760			08	rose
◇	761	□	◹†	06	lt rose
E	775			0128	vy lt blue
✳	801			0359	brown
3	822	□		0390	vy lt beige
	838		◹★	0380	dk brown
	869		◹★	0906	golden brown
	924		◹+	0851	dk grey blue
◆	926	◣		0850	grey blue
N	927	◹		0849	lt grey blue
2	928	□		0847	vy lt grey blue
★	930		◹★	0922	dk blue
8	931			0921	blue
C	932			0920	lt blue
◆	948			0892	lt peach
◼	3022		◹†	8581	grey
⊙	3024	◹		0900	lt grey
4	3042		◹★	0870	lt lavender
8	3045	◹		0888	dk gold
6	3046	◹		0887	gold
△	3047	□		0886	lt gold
	3328		◹+	011	dk rose
⊙	blanc			02	white Fr. Knot
⊙	838			0380	dk brown Fr. Knot
●	3041			0872	lavender Fr. Knot

LET'S PRETEND (144w x 121h)

	14 count	10⅜" x 8¾"
	16 count	9" x 7⅝"
	18 count	8" x 6¾"
	22 count	6⅝" x 5½"

Photo model stitched over two fabric threads on Cream Belfast Linen (32 ct) using 2 strands of embroidery floss for Cross Stitch and 1 strand for Backstitch and French Knots — approx design size 9" x 7⅝".

Grey area indicates last row of left side of design

★ Vy dk grey brown for chair only. Golden brown for hat and wallpaper crack only. Lt lavender for petticoat trim only. Green for all other.

+ Lt tan for reflection of frame in mirror only. Grey brown for reflection of chair in mirror only. Dk grey blue for bottle, reflection of bottle in mirror, and hatbox only. Dk rose for flowers on hat only. Beige for all other.

* Dk blue green for ribbons on hat and dress only. Dk beige for pantaloons only. Dk blue for chair cushions only. Dk brown for all other.

† Lt rose for reflection of wallpaper in mirror only. Grey for all other.

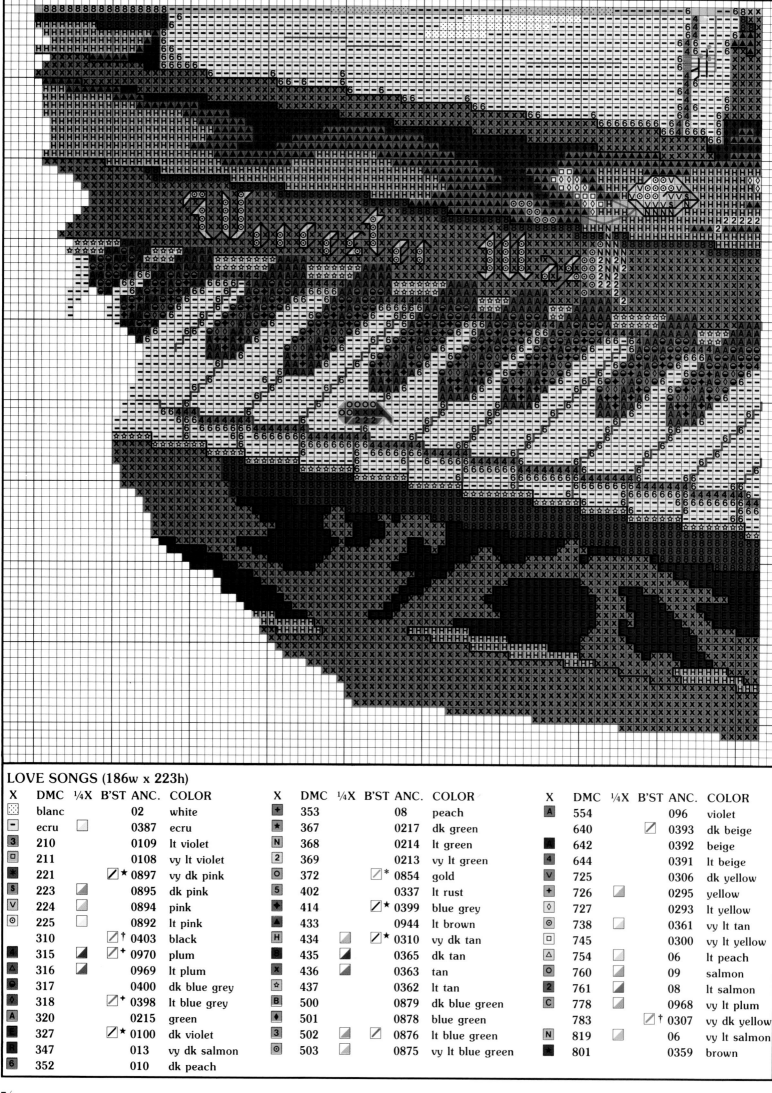

LOVE SONGS (186w x 223h)

X	DMC	¼X	B'ST	ANC.	COLOR
⁘	blanc			02	white
-	ecru	◩		0387	ecru
3	210			0109	lt violet
◻	211			0108	vy lt violet
✱	221		◩ ★	0897	vy dk pink
S	223	◩		0895	dk pink
V	224	◩		0894	pink
⊙	225	◩		0892	lt pink
	310		◩ †	0403	black
4	315	◩	◩ +	0970	plum
△	316	◩		0969	lt plum
◒	317			0400	dk blue grey
◊	318		◩ +	0398	lt blue grey
A	320			0215	green
E	327		◩ ★	0100	dk violet
R	347			013	vy dk salmon
6	352			010	dk peach
+	353			08	peach
★	367			0217	dk green
N	368			0214	lt green
2	369			0213	vy lt green
O	372		◩ *	0854	gold
5	402			0337	lt rust
✦	414		◩ ★	0399	blue grey
▲	433			0944	lt brown
H	434	◩	◩ ★	0310	vy dk tan
8	435	◩		0365	dk tan
X	436	◩		0363	tan
☆	437			0362	lt tan
B	500			0879	dk blue green
♦	501			0878	blue green
3	502	◩	◩	0876	lt blue green
⊙	503	◩		0875	vy lt blue green
A	554			096	violet
	640		◩	0393	dk beige
A	642			0392	beige
4	644			0391	lt beige
V	725			0306	dk yellow
+	726	◩		0295	yellow
◊	727			0293	lt yellow
⊙	738	◩		0361	vy lt tan
◻	745			0300	vy lt yellow
△	754	◩		06	lt peach
O	760	◩		09	salmon
2	761	◩		08	lt salmon
C	778	◩		0968	vy lt plum
	783		◩ †	0307	vy dk yellow
N	819	◩		06	vy lt salmon
✱	801			0359	brown

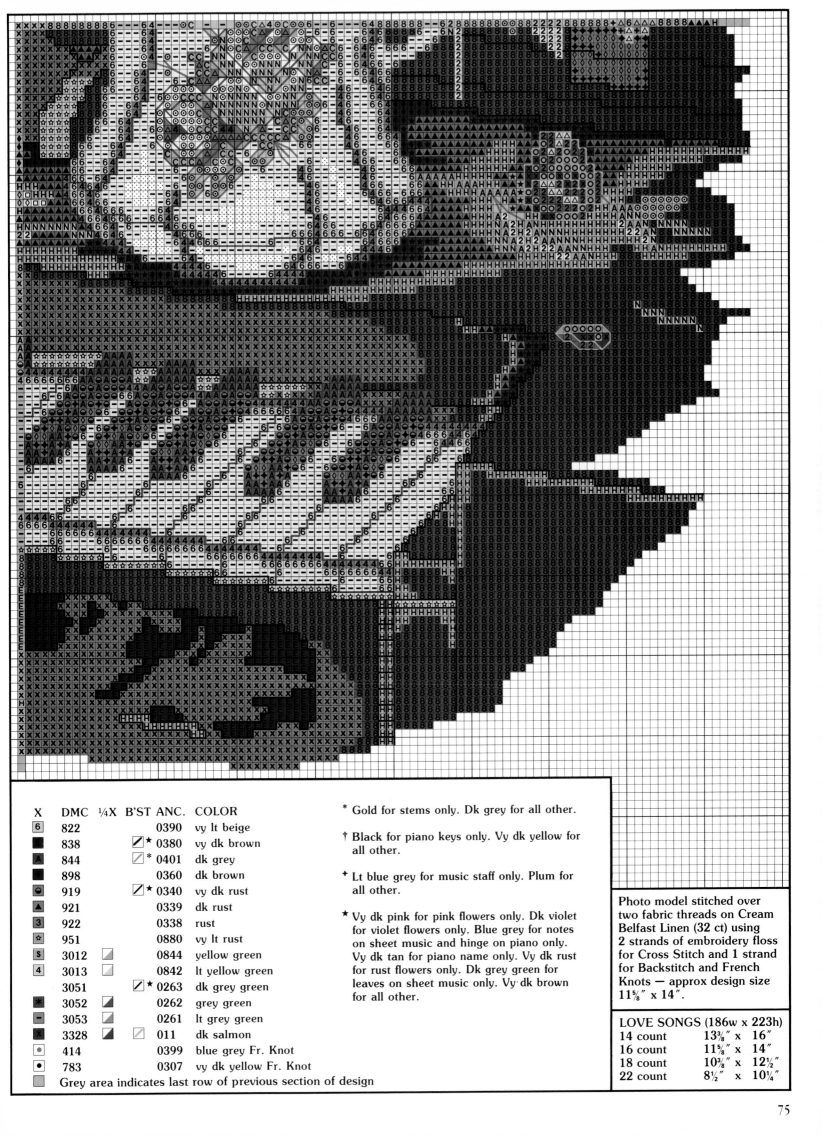

X	DMC	¼X	B'ST	ANC.	COLOR
6	822			0390	vy lt beige
■	838		◨★	0380	vy dk brown
▲	844		◨*	0401	dk grey
◆	898			0360	dk brown
◉	919		◨★	0340	vy dk rust
▲	921			0339	dk rust
3	922			0338	rust
☆	951			0880	vy lt rust
S	3012	◨		0844	yellow green
4	3013	◨		0842	lt yellow green
	3051		◨★	0263	dk grey green
✳	3052	◨		0262	grey green
−	3053	◨		0261	lt grey green
✕	3328	◨	◨	011	dk salmon
⊙	414			0399	blue grey Fr. Knot
●	783			0307	vy dk yellow Fr. Knot
▨	Grey area indicates last row of previous section of design				

* Gold for stems only. Dk grey for all other.

† Black for piano keys only. Vy dk yellow for all other.

⁺ Lt blue grey for music staff only. Plum for all other.

★ Vy dk pink for pink flowers only. Dk violet for violet flowers only. Blue grey for notes on sheet music and hinge on piano only. Vy dk tan for piano name only. Vy dk rust for rust flowers only. Dk grey green for leaves on sheet music only. Vy dk brown for all other.

Photo model stitched over two fabric threads on Cream Belfast Linen (32 ct) using 2 strands of embroidery floss for Cross Stitch and 1 strand for Backstitch and French Knots — approx design size 11⅝" x 14".

LOVE SONGS (186w x 223h)
14 count	13⅜"	x	16"
16 count	11⅝"	x	14"
18 count	10⅜"	x	12½"
22 count	8½"	x	10¼"

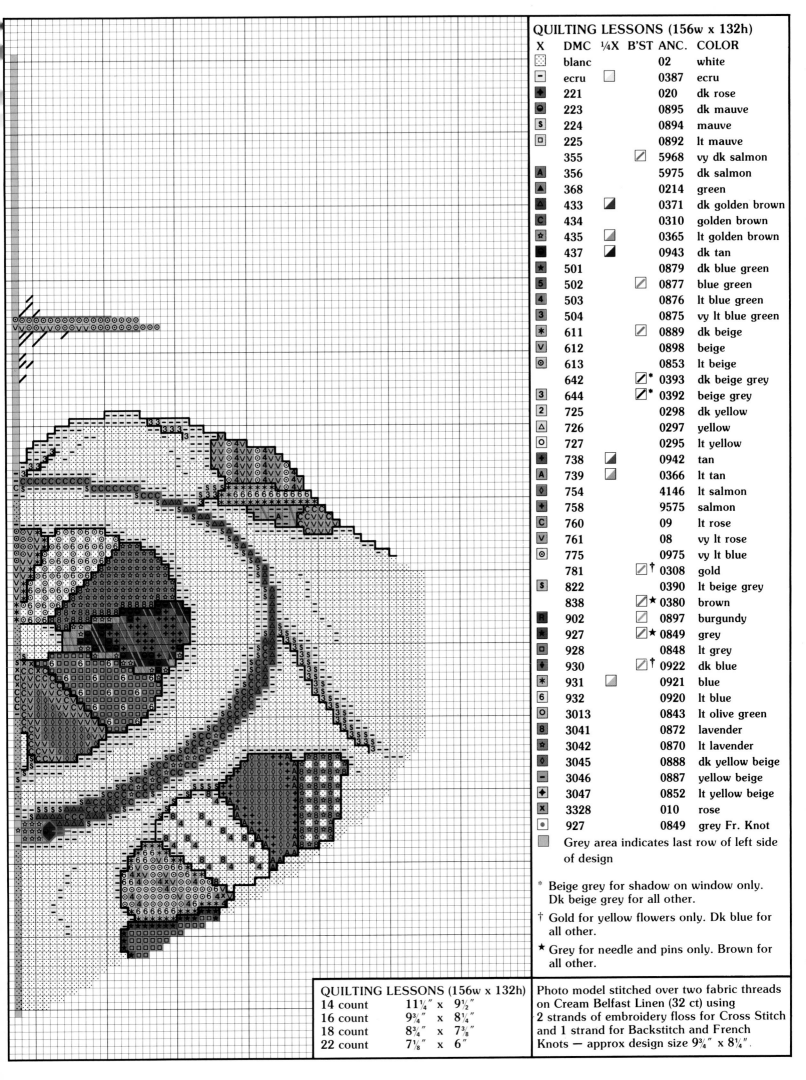

QUILTING LESSONS (156w x 132h)

X	DMC	¼X	B'ST	ANC.	COLOR
⣿	blanc			02	white
-	ecru	☐		0387	ecru
✦	221			020	dk rose
◉	223			0895	dk mauve
S	224			0894	mauve
□	225			0892	lt mauve
	355		╱	5968	vy dk salmon
A	356			5975	dk salmon
▲	368			0214	green
△	433	◪		0371	dk golden brown
C	434			0310	golden brown
☆	435	◪		0365	lt golden brown
■	437	◪		0943	dk tan
★	501			0879	dk blue green
5	502		╱	0877	blue green
4	503			0876	lt blue green
3	504			0875	vy lt blue green
✳	611		╱	0889	dk beige
V	612			0898	beige
◉	613			0853	lt beige
	642		╱*	0393	dk beige grey
3	644		╱*	0392	beige grey
2	725			0298	dk yellow
△	726			0297	yellow
◯	727			0295	lt yellow
✦	738	◪		0942	tan
A	739	◪		0366	lt tan
◇	754			4146	lt salmon
✦	758			9575	salmon
C	760			09	lt rose
V	761			08	vy lt rose
◉	775			0975	vy lt blue
	781		╱†	0308	gold
S	822			0390	lt beige grey
	838		╱★	0380	brown
R	902		╱	0897	burgundy
✱	927		╱★	0849	grey
□	928			0848	lt grey
◆	930		╱†	0922	dk blue
✳	931	◪		0921	blue
6	932			0920	lt blue
◎	3013			0843	lt olive green
8	3041			0872	lavender
✿	3042			0870	lt lavender
◇	3045			0888	dk yellow beige
-	3046			0887	yellow beige
✦	3047			0852	lt yellow beige
X	3328			010	rose
◉	927			0849	grey Fr. Knot

▨ Grey area indicates last row of left side of design

* Beige grey for shadow on window only.
Dk beige grey for all other.

† Gold for yellow flowers only. Dk blue for all other.

★ Grey for needle and pins only. Brown for all other.

QUILTING LESSONS (156w x 132h)

14 count	11¼"	x	9½"
16 count	9¾"	x	8¼"
18 count	8¾"	x	7⅜"
22 count	7⅛"	x	6"

Photo model stitched over two fabric threads on Cream Belfast Linen (32 ct) using 2 strands of embroidery floss for Cross Stitch and 1 strand for Backstitch and French Knots — approx design size 9¾" x 8¼".

Photo model stitched over two fabric threads on Cream Belfast Linen (32 ct) using 2 strands of embroidery floss for Cross Stitch and

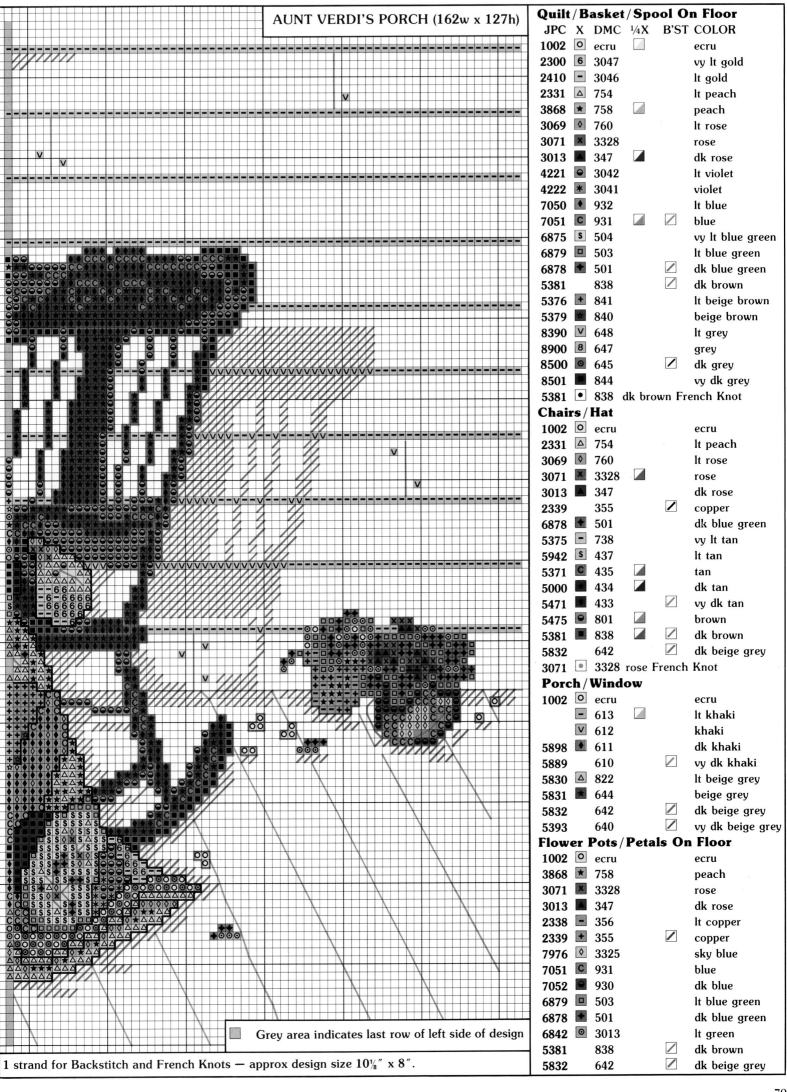

AUNT VERDI'S PORCH (162w x 127h)

Grey area indicates last row of left side of design

1 strand for Backstitch and French Knots — approx design size 10⅛″ x 8″.

Quilt / Basket / Spool On Floor

JPC	X	DMC	¼X	B'ST	COLOR
1002	○	ecru	☐		ecru
2300	6	3047			vy lt gold
2410	-	3046			lt gold
2331	△	754			lt peach
3868	★	758	◪		peach
3069	◇	760			lt rose
3071	✕	3328			rose
3013	▲	347	◪		dk rose
4221	⊖	3042			lt violet
4222	✳	3041			violet
7050	◆	932			lt blue
7051	C	931	◪	◪	blue
6875	S	504			vy lt blue green
6879	▢	503			lt blue green
6878	✦	501		◪	dk blue green
5381		838		◪	dk brown
5376	✚	841			lt beige brown
5379	✿	840			beige brown
8390	V	648			lt grey
8900	8	647			grey
8500	⊙	645		◪	dk grey
8501	■	844			vy dk grey
5381	●	838	dk brown French Knot		

Chairs / Hat

JPC	X	DMC	¼X	B'ST	COLOR
1002	○	ecru			ecru
2331	△	754			lt peach
3069	◇	760			lt rose
3071	✕	3328	◪		rose
3013	▲	347			dk rose
2339		355		◪	copper
6878	✦	501			dk blue green
5375	-	738			vy lt tan
5942	S	437			lt tan
5371	C	435	◪		tan
5000	✖	434	◪		dk tan
5471	▣	433		◪	vy dk tan
5475	⊙	801	◪		brown
5381	■	838	◪	◪	dk brown
5832		642		◪	dk beige grey
3071	⊙	3328	rose French Knot		

Porch / Window

JPC	X	DMC	¼X	B'ST	COLOR
1002	○	ecru			ecru
	-	613	◪		lt khaki
	V	612			khaki
5898	◆	611			dk khaki
5889		610		◪	vy dk khaki
5830	△	822			lt beige grey
5831	★	644			beige grey
5832		642		◪	dk beige grey
5393		640		◪	vy dk beige grey

Flower Pots / Petals On Floor

JPC	X	DMC	¼X	B'ST	COLOR
1002	○	ecru			ecru
3868	★	758			peach
3071	✕	3328			rose
3013	▲	347			dk rose
2338	-	356			lt copper
2339	✚	355		◪	copper
7976	◇	3325			sky blue
7051	C	931			blue
7052	⊙	930			dk blue
6879	▢	503			lt blue green
6878	✦	501			dk blue green
6842	⊙	3013			lt green
5381		838		◪	dk brown
5832		642		◪	dk beige grey

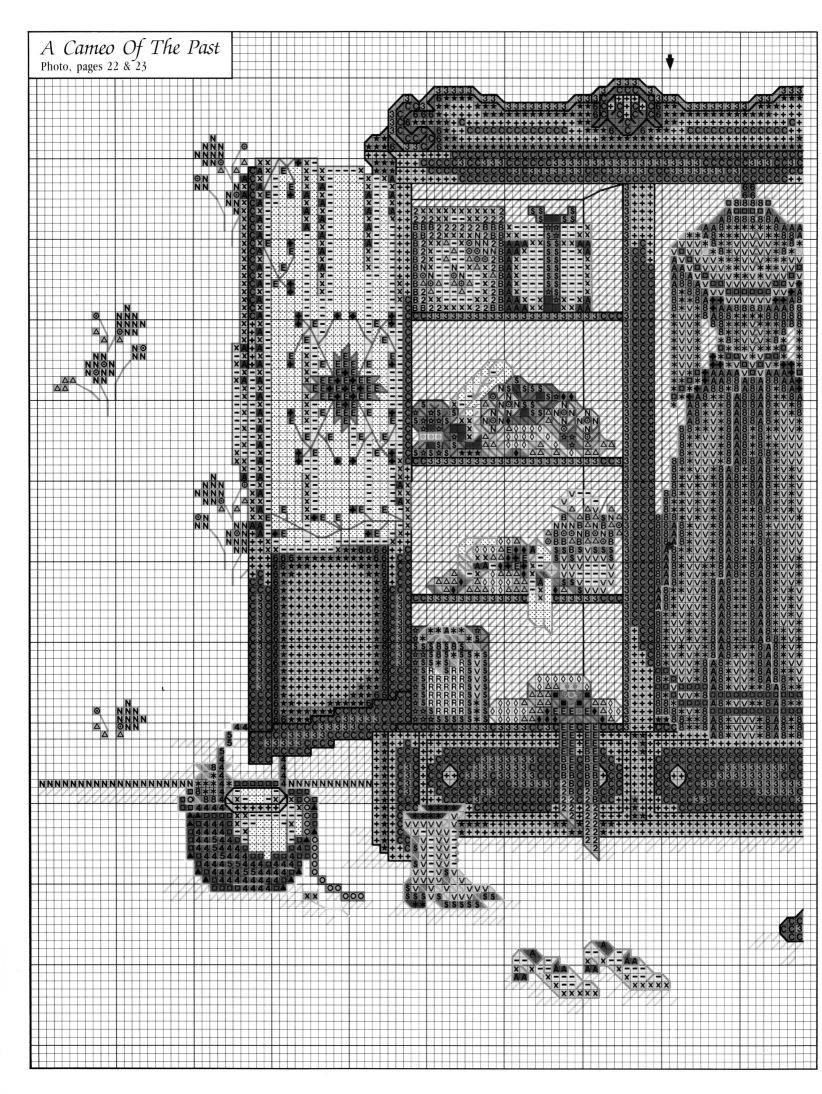

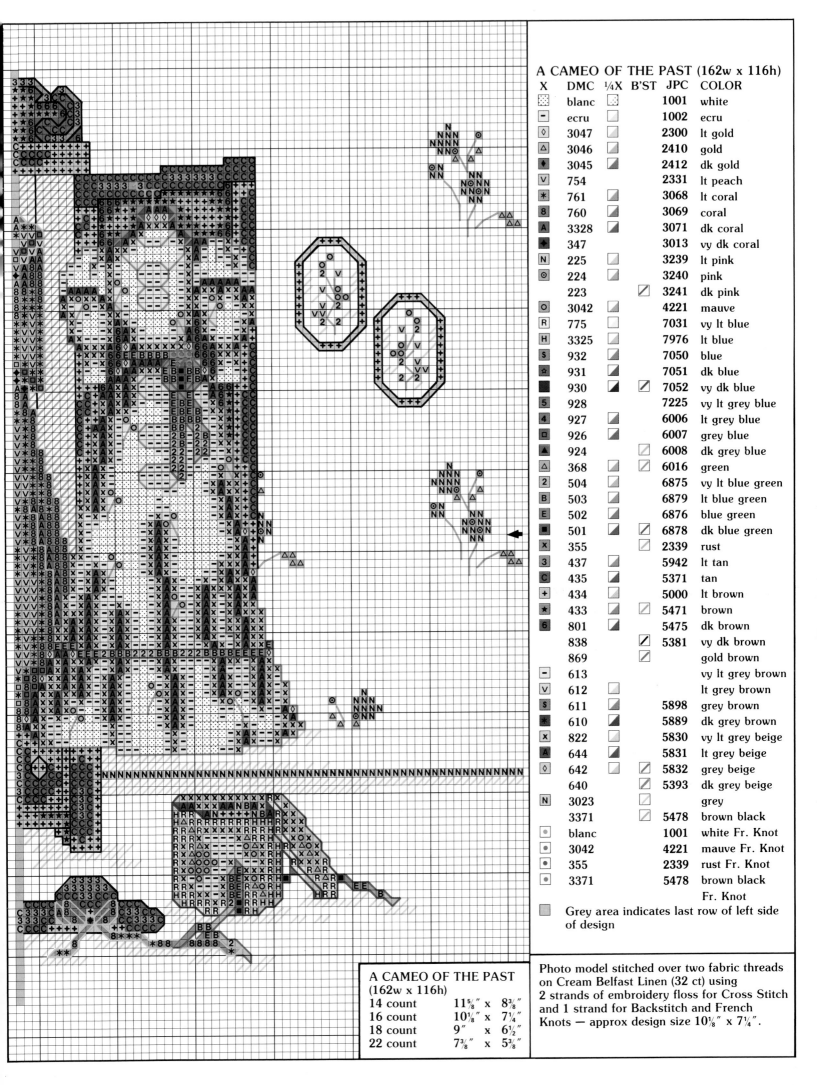

A CAMEO OF THE PAST (162w x 116h)

X	DMC	¼X	B'ST	JPC	COLOR
	blanc			1001	white
-	ecru			1002	ecru
◇	3047			2300	lt gold
△	3046			2410	gold
◆	3045			2412	dk gold
V	754			2331	lt peach
*	761			3068	lt coral
8	760			3069	coral
A	3328			3071	dk coral
✦	347			3013	vy dk coral
N	225			3239	lt pink
⊙	224			3240	pink
	223			3241	dk pink
O	3042			4221	mauve
R	775			7031	vy lt blue
H	3325			7976	lt blue
S	932			7050	blue
☆	931			7051	dk blue
■	930			7052	vy dk blue
5	928			7225	vy lt grey blue
4	927			6006	lt grey blue
□	926			6007	grey blue
▲	924			6008	dk grey blue
△	368			6016	green
2	504			6875	vy lt blue green
B	503			6879	lt blue green
E	502			6876	blue green
■	501			6878	dk blue green
X	355			2339	rust
3	437			5942	lt tan
C	435			5371	tan
+	434			5000	lt brown
★	433			5471	brown
6	801			5475	dk brown
	838			5381	vy dk brown
	869				gold brown
-	613				vy lt grey brown
V	612				lt grey brown
S	611			5898	grey brown
✳	610			5889	dk grey brown
X	822			5830	vy lt grey beige
A	644			5831	lt grey beige
◇	642			5832	grey beige
	640			5393	dk grey beige
N	3023				grey
	3371			5478	brown black
⊙	blanc			1001	white Fr. Knot
⊙	3042			4221	mauve Fr. Knot
⊙	355			2339	rust Fr. Knot
⊙	3371			5478	brown black Fr. Knot

▢ Grey area indicates last row of left side of design

A CAMEO OF THE PAST
(162w x 116h)

14 count	11⅝" x	8⅜"
16 count	10⅛" x	7¼"
18 count	9" x	6½"
22 count	7⅜" x	5⅜"

Photo model stitched over two fabric threads on Cream Belfast Linen (32 ct) using 2 strands of embroidery floss for Cross Stitch and 1 strand for Backstitch and French Knots — approx design size 10⅛" x 7¼".

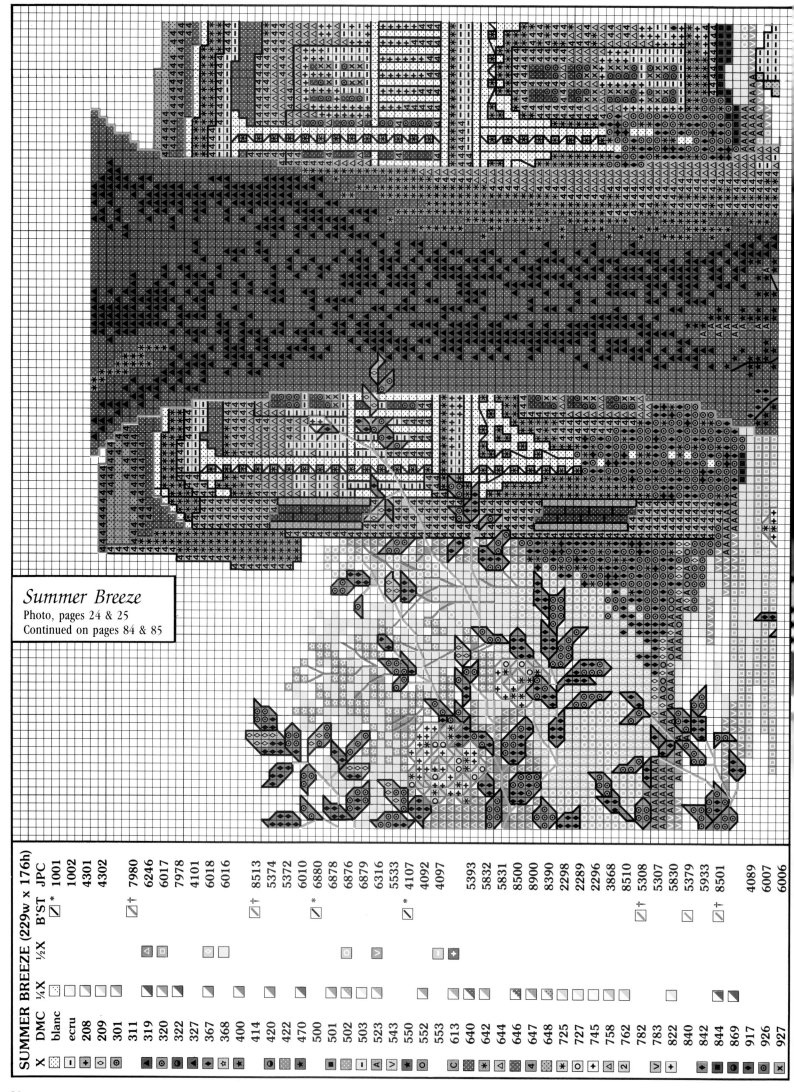

Summer Breeze
Photo, pages 24 & 25
Continued on pages 84 & 85

	2336		
	5395		
	8390		
	5388		
*	3883		
	7976		
	6266		
	3004		
	3003		
	4087		
	3089		

* Blanc for side windows. 500 for leaves, fern stems, flower stems in basket, grass, and shutters. 550 for purple irises and quilt. 3064 for flesh. 3787 for house, swing, arbor, and bucket handle.

† 311 for dress and bucket. 414 for white roses. 782 for yellow roses and yellow irises. 844 for background trees, swing chains, roof, windows, and hair.

×	950
	3021
	3022
	3023
	3024
	3033
	3064
	3325
	3347
	3350
	3354
	3607
	3685
	3731
	3733
	3755
	3768
	3773
	3787
	3790

Grey area indicates last row of previous section of design

Photo model stitched over two fabric threads on Cream Belfast Linen (32 ct) using 2 strands of embroidery floss for Cross Stitch, blanc Backstitch for side windows, and 844 Backstitch for swing chains, and 1 strand for Half Cross Stitch and all other Backstitch — approx design size 14⅜" x 11".

SUMMER BREEZE (229w x 176h)

14 count	16⅜" x 12⅝"
16 count	14⅜" x 11"
18 count	12¾" x 9⅞"
22 count	10½" x 8"

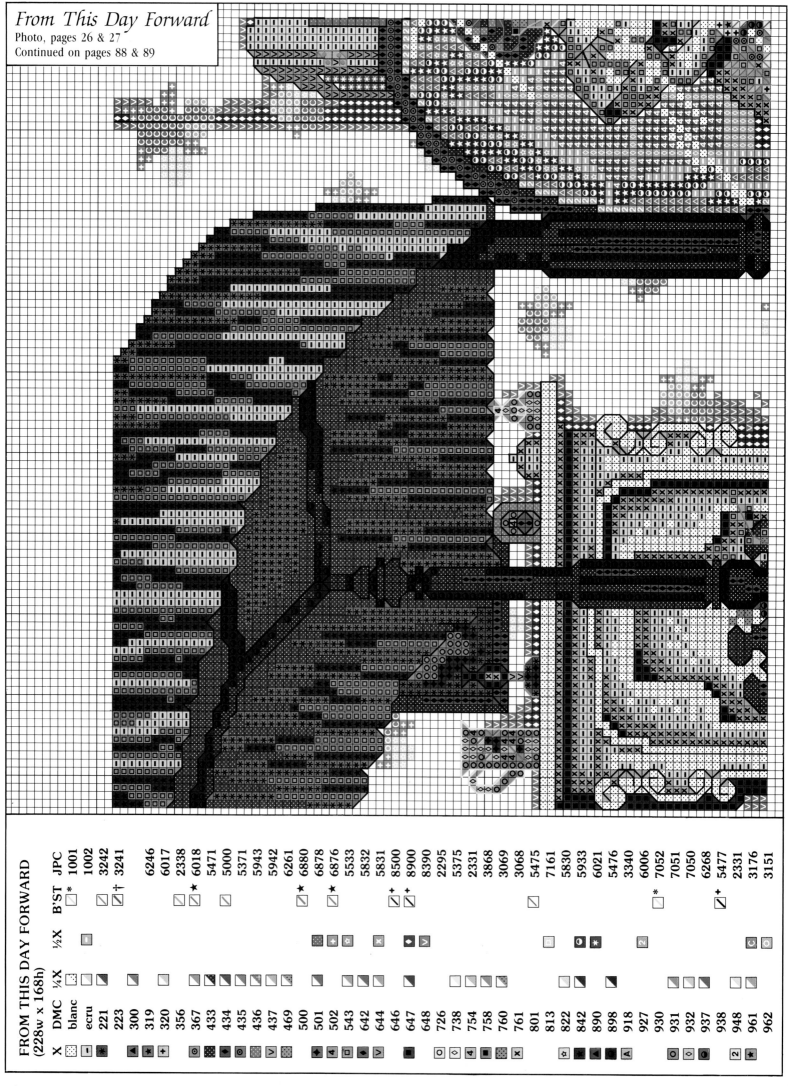

From This Day Forward

Photo, pages 26 & 27
Continued on pages 88 & 89

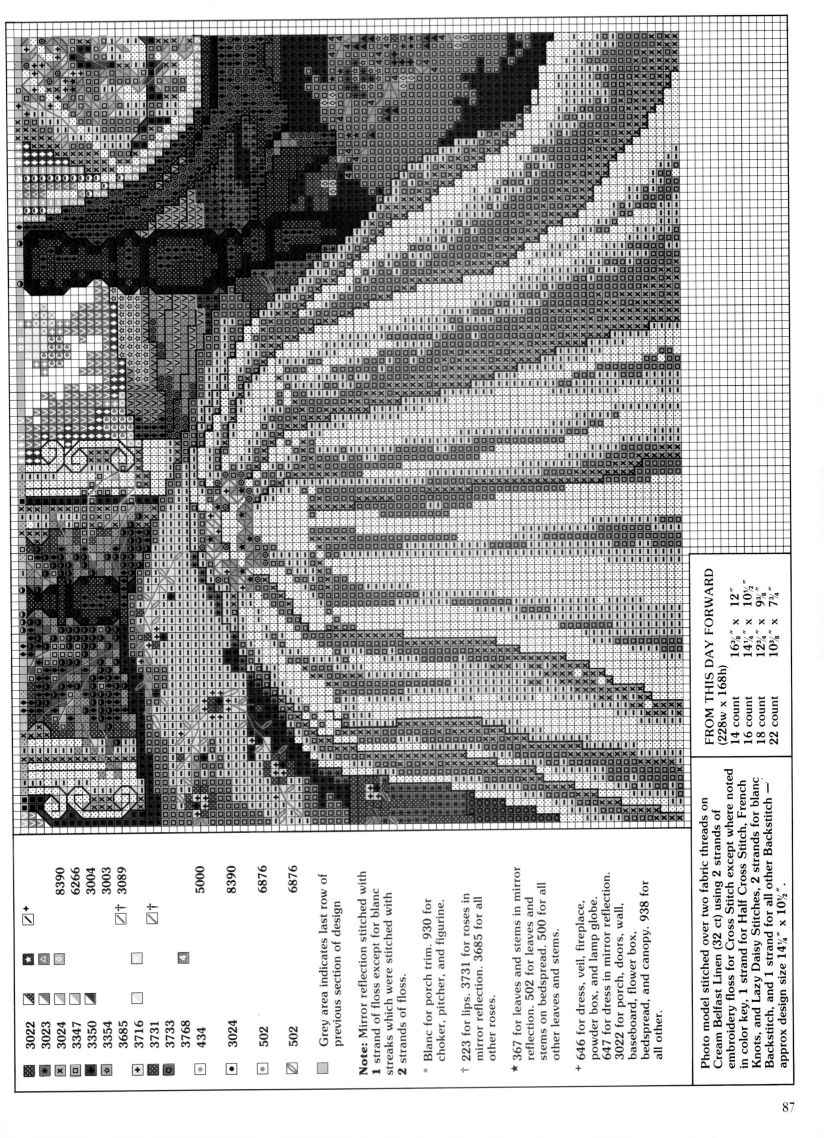

FROM THIS DAY FORWARD
(228w x 168h)

14 count	16⅜" x	12"
16 count	14¼" x	10½"
18 count	12¾" x	9⅜"
22 count	10⅜" x	7¼"

Color Key

3022
3023
3024
3347
3350
3354
3685
3716
3731
3733
3768
434
3024
502
502

⧄+
8390
6266
3004
3003
⧄† 3089
⧄†

5000

8390

6876

6876

Grey area indicates last row of previous section of design

Note: Mirror reflection stitched with **1** strand of floss except for blanc streaks which were stitched with **2** strands of floss.

* Blanc for porch trim. 930 for choker, pitcher, and figurine.

† 223 for lips. 3731 for roses in mirror reflection. 3685 for all other roses.

★ 367 for leaves and stems in mirror reflection. 502 for leaves and stems on bedspread. 500 for all other leaves and stems.

+ 646 for dress, veil, fireplace, powder box, and lamp globe. 647 for dress in mirror reflection. 3022 for porch, doors, wall, baseboard, flower box, bedspread, and canopy. 938 for all other.

Photo model stitched over two fabric threads on Cream Belfast Linen (32 ct) using 2 strands of embroidery floss for Cross Stitch except where noted in color key, 1 strand for Half Cross Stitch, French Knots, and Lazy Daisy Stitches, 2 strands for blanc Backstitch, and 1 strand for all other Backstitch — approx design size 14¼" x 10½".

87

SPRING REMEMBERED (162w x 127h)

X	DMC	¼X	½X	B'ST	JPC	COLOR
▦	blanc				1001	white
◇	ecru	□			1002	ecru
▦	225	◪			3066	pink
✳	320	◿			6017	green
◆	347	◿			3013	dk salmon
	355			◿	2339	rust
	367			◿*	6018	dk green
▦	368	◪	△	◿	6016	lt green
✕	369	◿			6015	vy lt green
E	372					khaki
N	422				5372	hazel brown
▲	433				5471	lt brown
▦	434	◿			5000	vy dk tan
★	435	◿			5371	dk tan
▦	436	◿	⊟		5943	tan
⊙	437	□			5942	lt tan
■	500	◢			6880	vy dk blue green
✳	501			◿†	6878	dk blue green
▢	502	◿	○		6876	blue green
✚	503	◿			6879	lt blue green
☆	504				6875	vy lt blue green
R	552				4092	purple
	640			◿*	5393	dk beige
◆	644				5831	beige
✚	676	□	✦		2874	gold
✳	729	◿			2875	dk gold
▦	738				5375	vy lt tan
4	760	◿	☆		3069	lt salmon
2	761	□			3068	vy lt salmon
▦	801			◿★	5475	brown
☆	822				5830	lt beige
■	838			◿★	5381	dk brown
	869			◿*		dk hazel brown
▦	930	◢		◿†	7052	vy dk blue
▦	931	◢			7051	dk blue
4	932	◿			7050	blue
C	3013				6842	yellow green
V	3032	◿			5393	taupe
✕	3033	□			5388	lt taupe
A	3041		▢		4222	violet
O	3042		◇		4221	lt violet
◆	3045				2412	dk yellow biege
▢	3046	◿			2410	yellow beige
▦	3047	◪			2300	lt yellow beige
△	3328	◿		◿	3071	salmon
◉	3740					dk violet
△	3743					vy lt violet
2	3752	◿			7876	lt blue
▢	3753	□				vy lt blue
	3790			◿*		dk taupe

▦ Grey area indicates last row of right side of design.

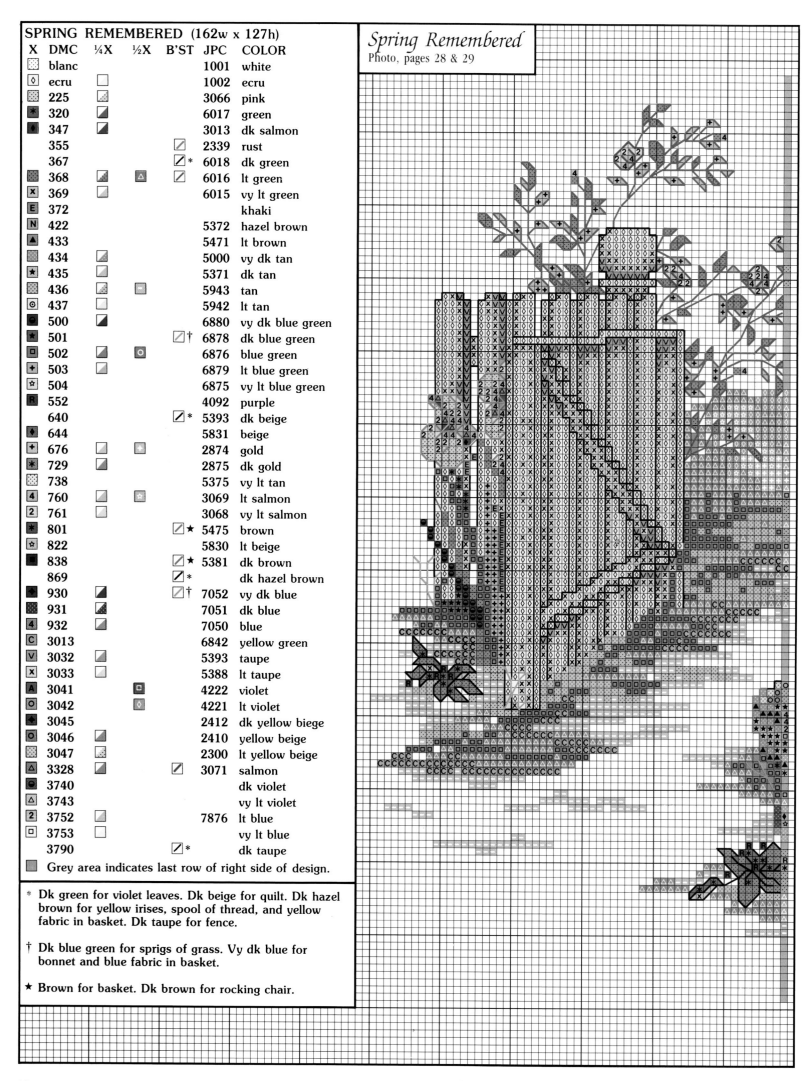

* Dk green for violet leaves. Dk beige for quilt. Dk hazel brown for yellow irises, spool of thread, and yellow fabric in basket. Dk taupe for fence.

† Dk blue green for sprigs of grass. Vy dk blue for bonnet and blue fabric in basket.

★ Brown for basket. Dk brown for rocking chair.

Photo model stitched over two fabric threads on Cream Belfast Linen (32 ct) using 2 strands of embroidery floss for Cross Stitch and 1 strand for Half Cross Stitch and Backstitch — approx design size 10⅛″ x 8″.

SPRING REMEMBERED
(162w x 127h)

14 count	11⅝″	x	9⅛″
16 count	10⅛″	x	8″
18 count	9″	x	7⅛″
22 count	7⅜″	x	5⅞″

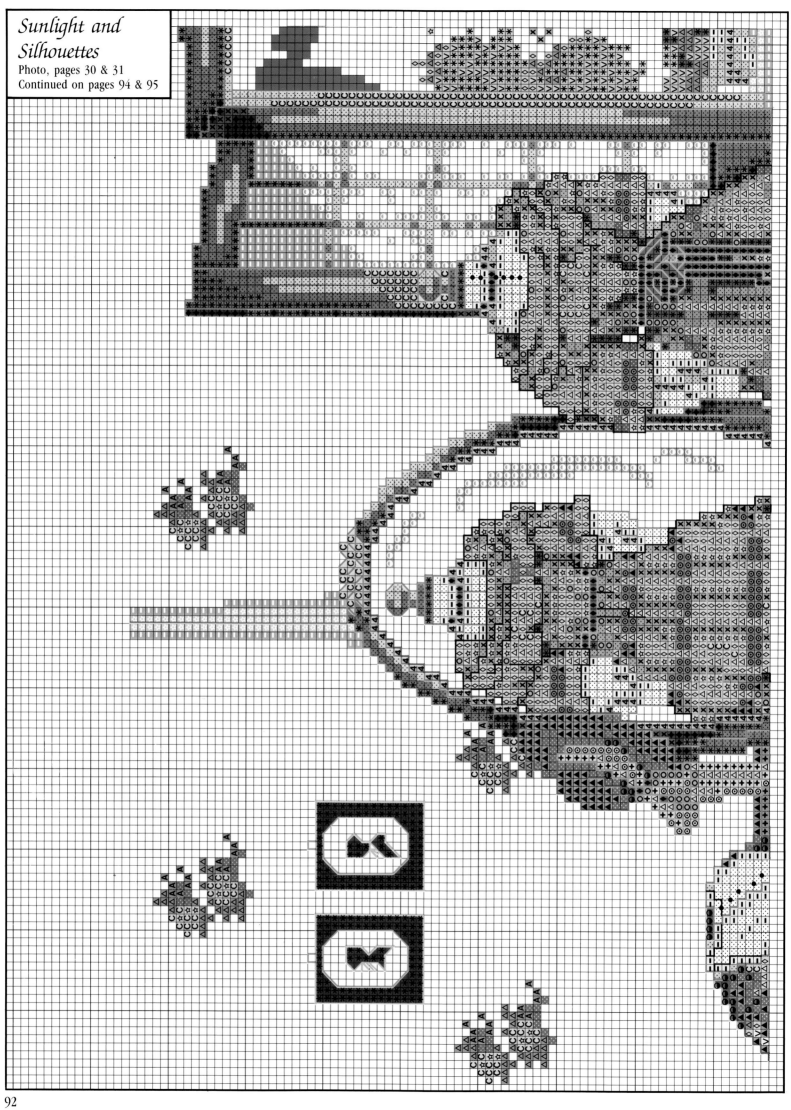

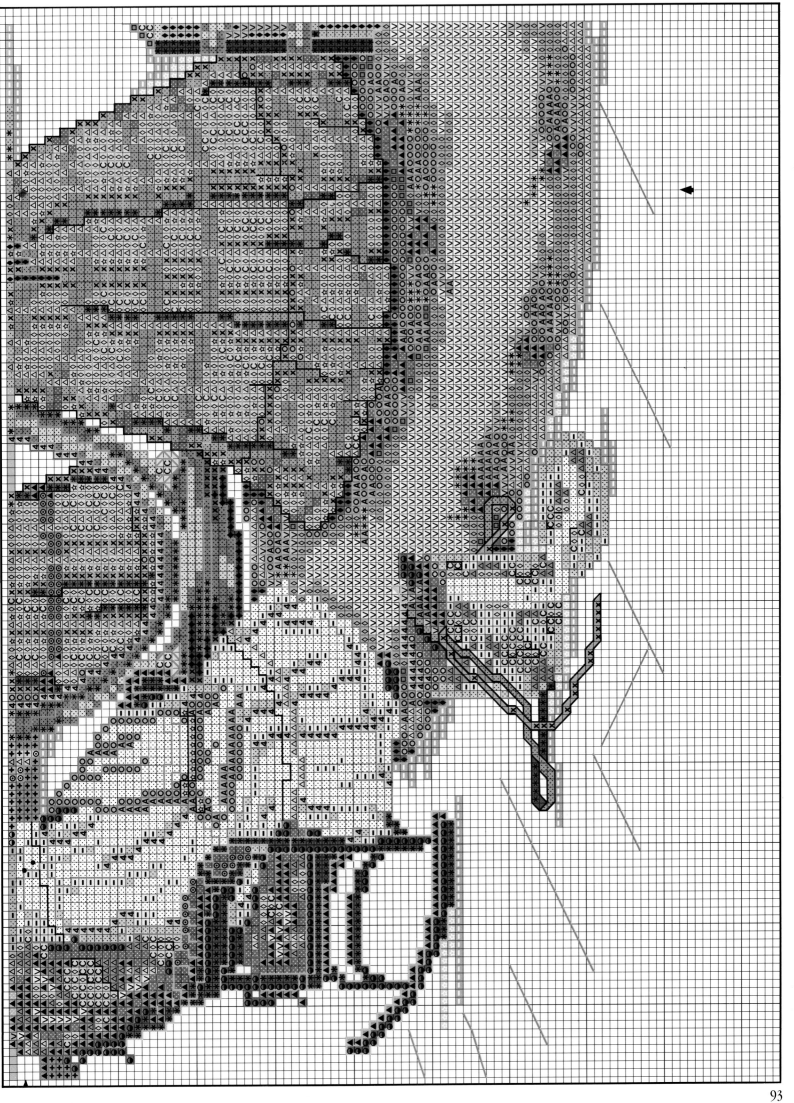

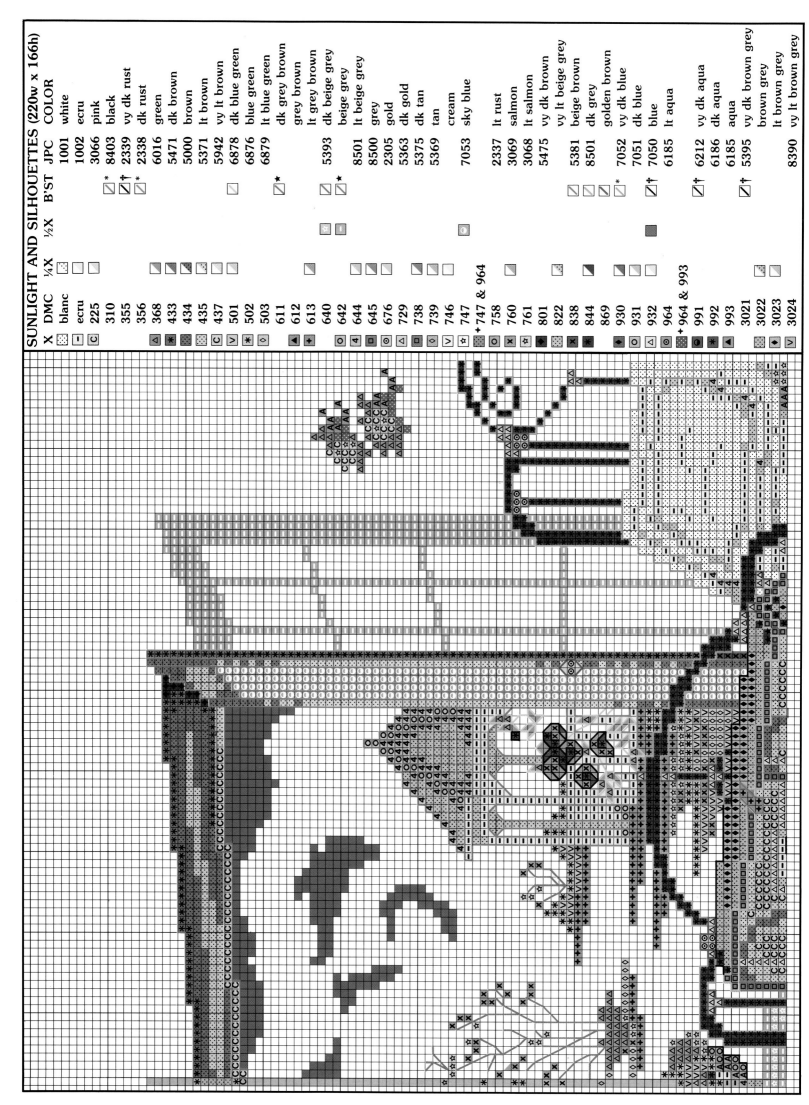

SUNLIGHT AND SILHOUETTES (220w x 166h)

X	DMC	B'ST	½X	¼X	JPC	COLOR
	blanc				1001	white
	ecru				1002	ecru
	225				3066	pink
	310	*			8403	black
	355	†			2339	vy dk rust
	356	*			2338	dk rust
	368				6016	green
	433				5471	dk brown
	434				5000	brown
	435				5371	lt brown
	437				5942	vy lt brown
	501				6878	dk blue green
	502				6876	blue green
	503				6879	lt blue green
	611	★				dk grey brown
	612					grey brown
	613					lt grey brown
	640	★			5393	dk beige grey
	642					beige grey
	644				8501	lt beige grey
	645				8500	grey
	676				2305	gold
	729				5363	dk gold
	738				5375	dk tan
	739				5369	tan
	746					cream
	747				7053	sky blue
	+747 & 964					
	758				2337	lt rust
	760				3069	salmon
	761				3068	lt salmon
	801				5475	vy dk brown
	822					vy lt beige grey
	838				5381	beige brown
	844				8501	dk grey
	869					golden brown
	930	*			7052	vy dk blue
	931				7051	dk blue
	932	†			7050	blue
	964				6185	lt aqua
	+964 & 993					
	991	†			6212	vy dk aqua
	992				6186	dk aqua
	993				6185	aqua
	3021	†			5395	vy dk brown grey
	3022					brown grey
	3023					lt brown grey
	3024				8390	vy lt brown grey

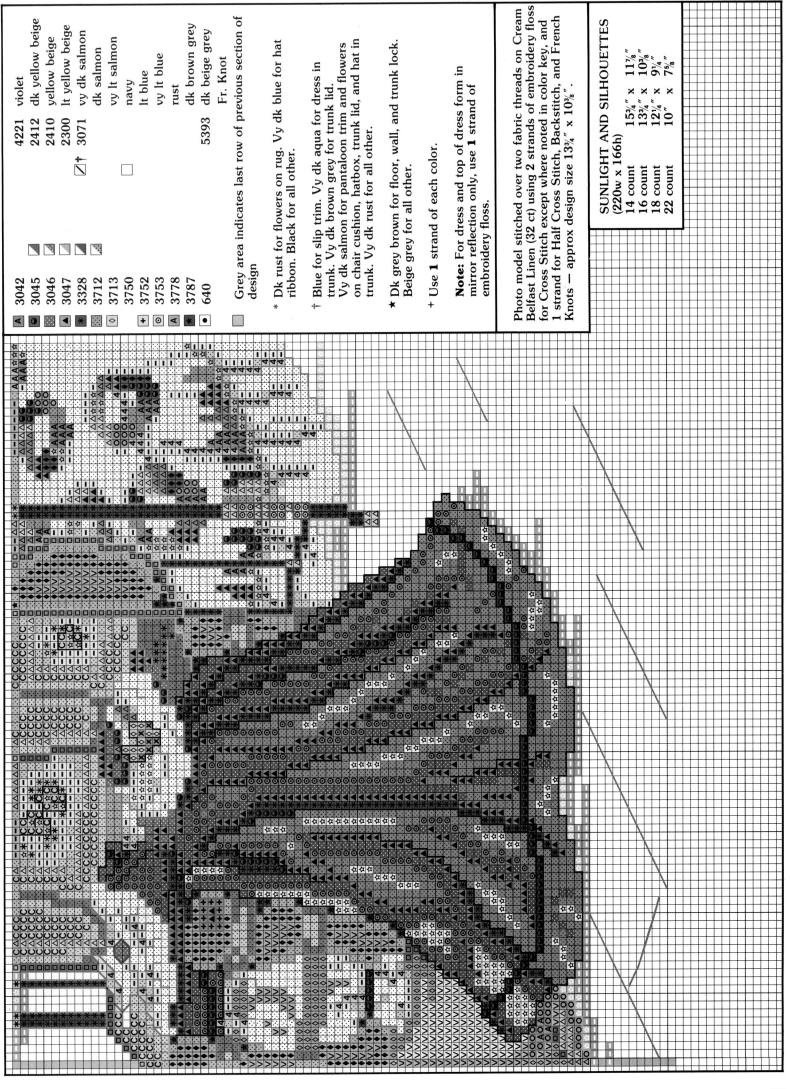

4221	violet
2412	dk yellow beige
2410	yellow beige
2300	lt yellow beige
3071	vy dk salmon
	dk salmon
	vy lt salmon
	navy
	lt blue
	vy lt blue
	rust
	dk brown grey
5393	dk beige grey
	Fr. Knot

3042	
3045	
3046	
3047	
3328	
3712	
3713	
3750	
3752	
3753	
3778	
3787	
640	

Grey area indicates last row of previous section of design

* Dk rust for flowers on rug. Vy dk blue for hat ribbon. Black for all other.

† Blue for slip trim. Vy dk aqua for dress in trunk. Vy dk brown grey for trunk lid. Vy dk salmon for pantaloon trim and flowers on chair cushion, hatbox, trunk lid, and hat in trunk. Vy dk rust for all other.

★ Dk grey brown for floor, wall, and trunk lock. Beige grey for all other.

+ Use **1** strand of each color.

Note: For dress and top of dress form in mirror reflection only, use **1** strand of embroidery floss.

Photo model stitched over two fabric threads on Cream Belfast Linen (32 ct) using **2** strands of embroidery floss for Cross Stitch except where noted in color key, and 1 strand for Half Cross Stitch, Backstitch, and French Knots — approx design size 13¾" x 10⅜".

SUNLIGHT AND SILHOUETTES
(220w x 166h)

14 count	15¾"	x	11⅞"
16 count	13¾"	x	10⅜"
18 count	12¼"	x	9¼"
22 count	10"	x	7⅝"

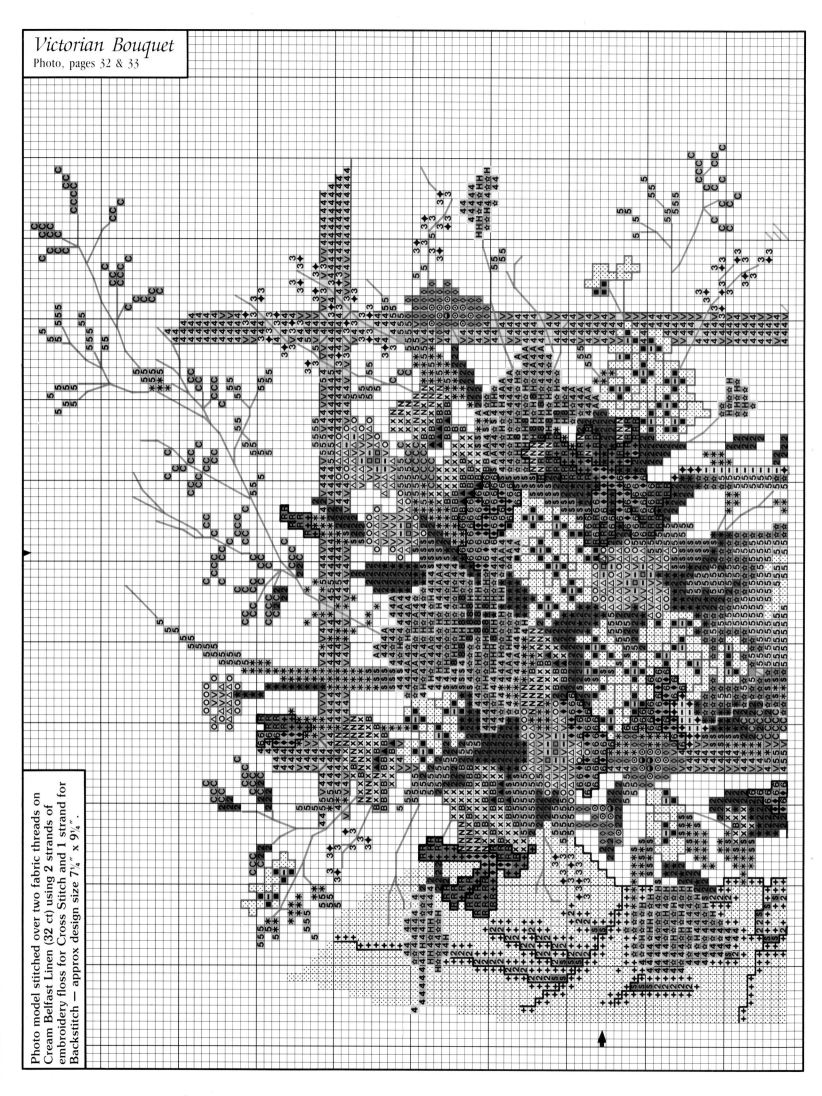

Photo model stitched over two fabric threads on Cream Belfast Linen (32 ct) using 2 strands of embroidery floss for Cross Stitch and 1 strand for Backstitch — approx design size 7¼" x 9¼".

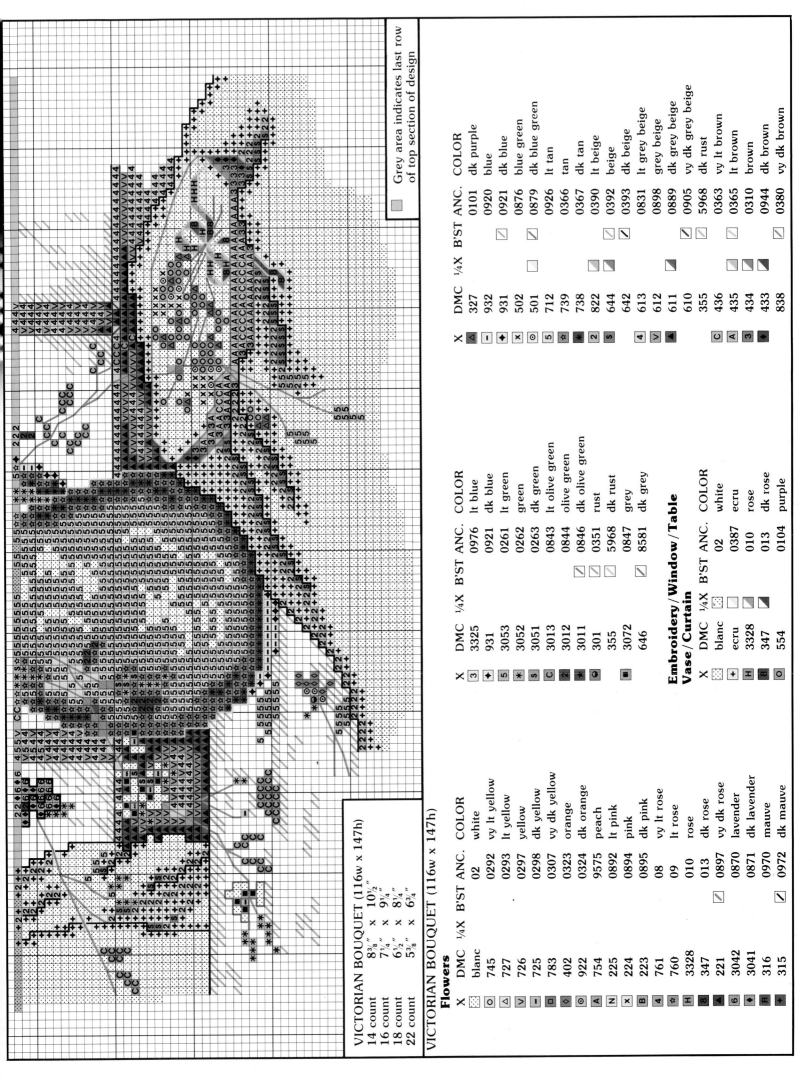

Grey area indicates last row of top section of design

VICTORIAN BOUQUET (116w x 147h)

14 count	8 3/8" x 10 1/2"
16 count	7 1/4" x 9 1/4"
18 count	6 1/2" x 8 1/4"
22 count	5 3/8" x 6 3/4"

VICTORIAN BOUQUET (116w x 147h)

Flowers

X	DMC	1/4X	B'ST	ANC.	COLOR
	blanc			02	white
	745			0292	vy lt yellow
	727			0293	lt yellow
	726			0297	yellow
	725			0298	dk yellow
	783			0307	vy dk yellow
	402			0323	orange
	922			0324	dk orange
	754			9575	peach
	225			0892	lt pink
	224			0894	pink
	223			0895	dk pink
	761			08	vy lt rose
	760			09	lt rose
	3328			010	rose
	347			013	dk rose
	221		◩	0897	vy dk rose
	3042			0870	lavender
	3041			0871	dk lavender
	316			0970	mauve
	315		◩	0972	dk mauve

X	DMC	1/4X	B'ST	ANC.	COLOR
	3325			0976	lt blue
	931			0921	dk blue
	3053			0261	lt green
	3052			0262	green
	3051			0263	dk green
	3013			0843	lt olive green
	3012			0844	olive green
	3011		◩	0846	dk olive green
	301		◩	0351	rust
	355		◩	5968	dk rust
	3072			0847	grey
	646		◩	8581	dk grey

Embroidery/Window/Table
Vase/Curtain

X	DMC	1/4X	B'ST	ANC.	COLOR
	blanc			02	white
	ecru			0387	ecru
	3328			010	rose
	347			013	dk rose
	554			0104	purple

X	DMC	1/4X	B'ST	ANC.	COLOR
	327			0101	dk purple
	932			0920	blue
	931		◩	0921	dk blue
	502			0876	blue green
	501		◩	0879	dk blue green
	712			0926	lt tan
	739			0366	tan
	738			0367	dk tan
	822			0390	lt beige
	644		◩	0392	beige
	642			0393	dk beige
	613			0831	lt grey beige
	612			0898	grey beige
	611		◩	0889	vy dk grey beige
	610			0905	dk grey
	355		◩	5968	dk rust
	436		◩	0363	vy lt brown
	435		◩	0365	lt brown
	434		◩	0310	brown
	433		◩	0944	dk brown
	838		◩	0380	vy dk brown

SISTERS THREE (174w x 123h)

X	DMC	¼X	½X	B'ST	JPC
	blanc				1001
−	ecru				1002
	221			∕ *	3242
V	223				3241
+	224				3240
	225				3066
	310			∕†	8403
	355			∕	2339
◊	368			∕ *	6016
◆	433				5471
	434				5000
8	435				5371
+	436				5943
	437				5942
	500			∕★	6880
✳	501				6878
⊙	502				6876
△	503				6879
☆	504				6875
	610			∕ *	
✳	611				
◊	612				
X	613				
	640			∕	5393
	642			∕	
	644				8501
V	645				8500
✳	646				8500
+	725				2298
O	738				5375
⊙	754				2331
★	760				3069
	761				3068
X	775				7031
	801				5475
O	822				
	838			∕ *	5381
■	844			∕†	8501
▲	926				6007
+	927				6006
◆	930			∕★	7052
⊙	931				7051
	932				7050
	939			∕ *	7160
	3022				
◊	3023				
⊙	3045				2412
	3046				2410
△	3047				2300
V	3325				7976
⊙	3328				3071
•	310	Fr. Knot			8403
•	501	Fr. Knot			6878
•	3328	Fr. Knot			3071

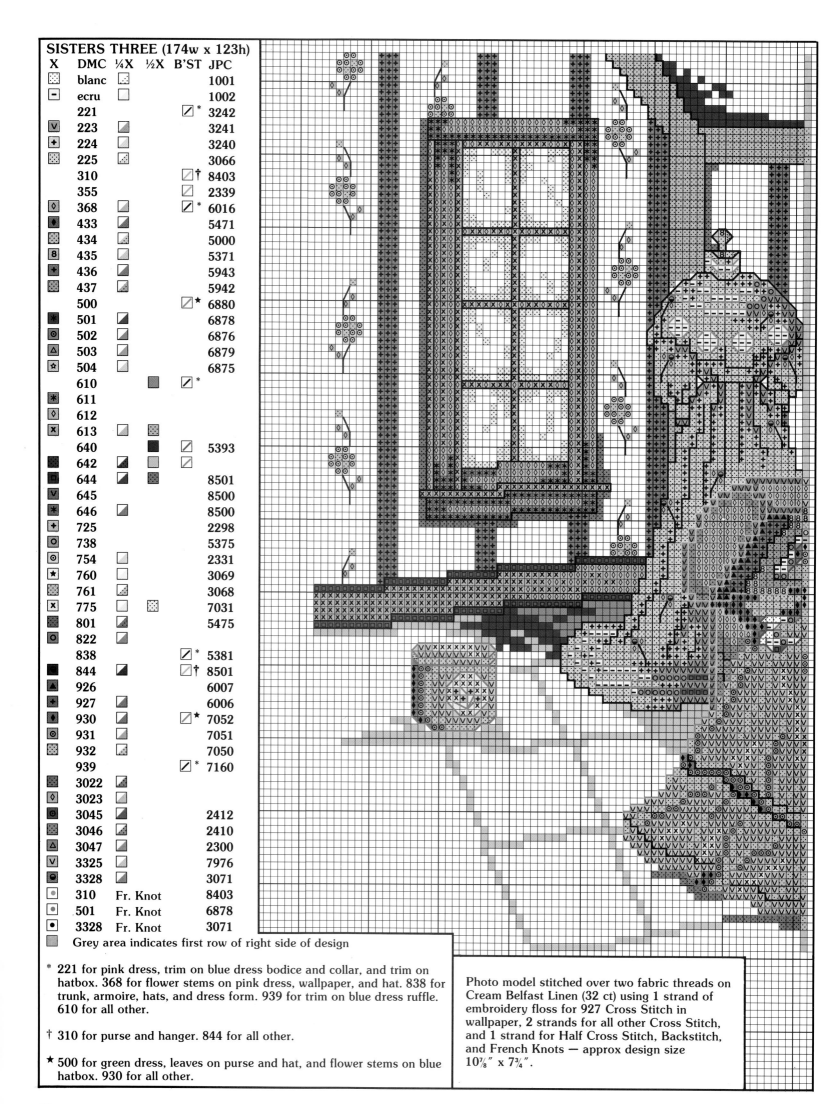

Grey area indicates first row of right side of design

* 221 for pink dress, trim on blue dress bodice and collar, and trim on hatbox. 368 for flower stems on pink dress, wallpaper, and hat. 838 for trunk, armoire, hats, and dress form. 939 for trim on blue dress ruffle. 610 for all other.

† 310 for purse and hanger. 844 for all other.

★ 500 for green dress, leaves on purse and hat, and flower stems on blue hatbox. 930 for all other.

Photo model stitched over two fabric threads on Cream Belfast Linen (32 ct) using 1 strand of embroidery floss for 927 Cross Stitch in wallpaper, 2 strands for all other Cross Stitch, and 1 strand for Half Cross Stitch, Backstitch, and French Knots — approx design size 10⅞″ x 7¾″.

SISTERS THREE (174w x 123h)

14 count	12½″	x	8⅞″
16 count	10⅞″	x	7¾″
18 count	9¾″	x	6⅞″
22 count	8″	x	5⅝″

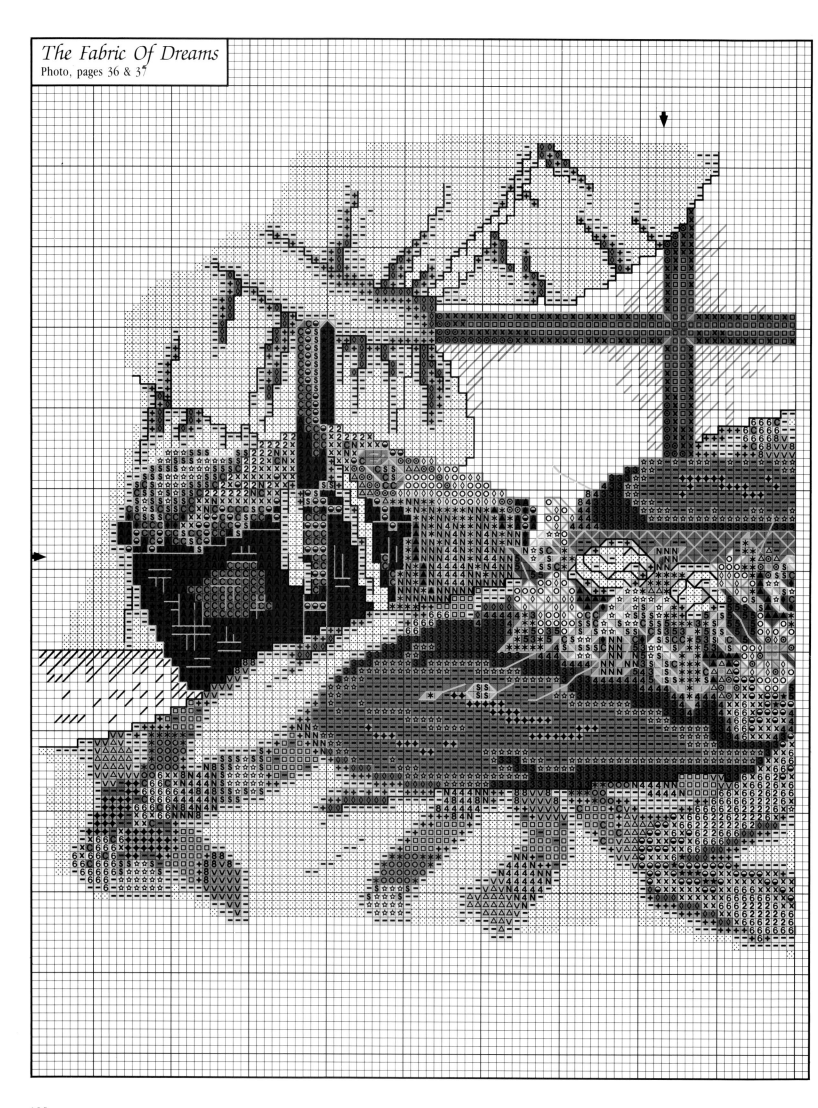

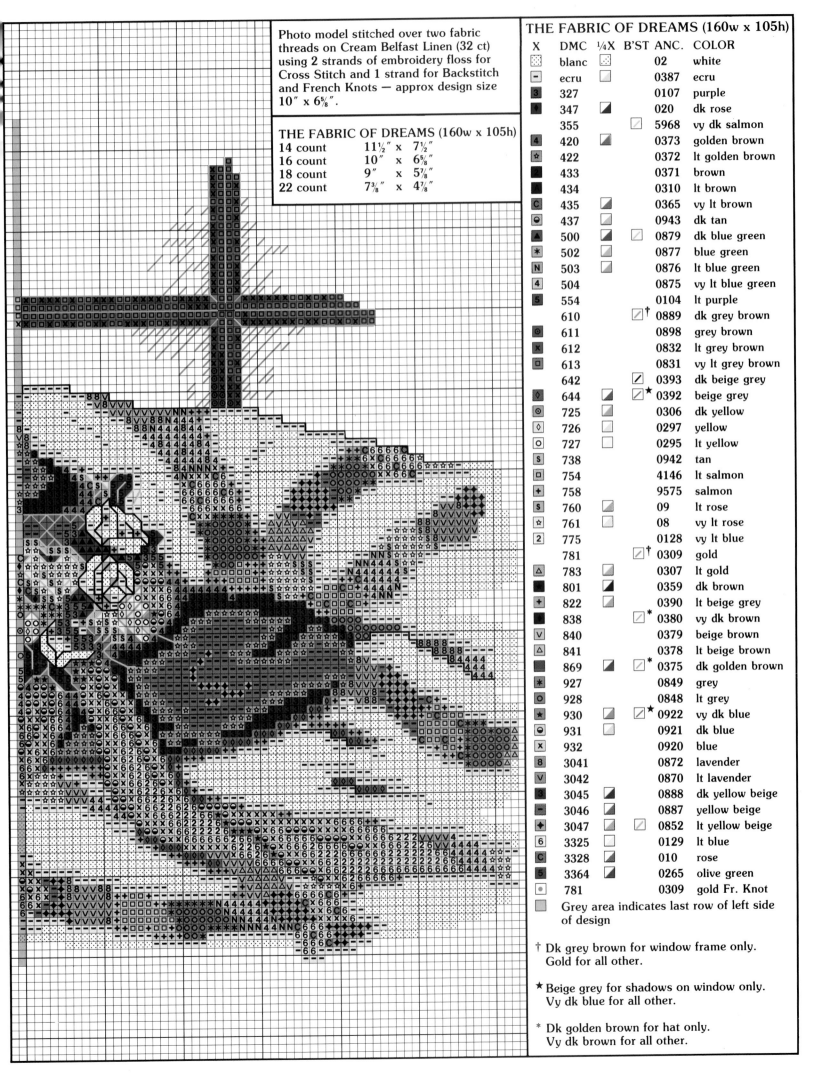

Photo model stitched over two fabric threads on Cream Belfast Linen (32 ct) using 2 strands of embroidery floss for Cross Stitch and 1 strand for Backstitch and French Knots — approx design size 10″ x 6⅝″.

THE FABRIC OF DREAMS (160w x 105h)

14 count	11½″	x 7½″
16 count	10″	x 6⅝″
18 count	9″	x 5⅞″
22 count	7⅜″	x 4⅞″

THE FABRIC OF DREAMS (160w x 105h)

X	DMC	¼X	B'ST	ANC.	COLOR
▢	blanc	▢		02	white
−	ecru			0387	ecru
3	327			0107	purple
◈	347	◣		020	dk rose
	355		◩	5968	vy dk salmon
4	420	◣		0373	golden brown
☆	422			0372	lt golden brown
2	433			0371	brown
◣	434			0310	lt brown
C	435	◣		0365	vy lt brown
⊙	437	◣		0943	dk tan
▲	500	◣	◩	0879	dk blue green
✳	502	◣		0877	blue green
N	503	◣		0876	lt blue green
4	504			0875	vy lt blue green
5	554			0104	lt purple
	610		◩†	0889	dk grey brown
⊙	611			0898	grey brown
X	612			0832	lt grey brown
▢	613			0831	vy lt grey brown
	642		◪	0393	dk beige grey
◇	644	◣	◩★	0392	beige grey
⊙	725	◣		0306	dk yellow
◇	726	◣		0297	yellow
O	727	▢		0295	lt yellow
S	738			0942	tan
▢	754			4146	lt salmon
+	758			9575	salmon
S	760	◣		09	lt rose
☆	761	▢		08	vy lt rose
2	775			0128	vy lt blue
△	781		◩†	0309	gold
△	783	◣		0307	lt gold
■	801	◣		0359	dk brown
+	822	◣		0390	lt beige grey
■	838		◩*	0380	vy dk brown
V	840			0379	beige brown
△	841			0378	lt beige brown
▣	869	◣	◩*	0375	dk golden brown
✳	927			0849	grey
O	928			0848	lt grey
★	930	◣	◩★	0922	vy dk blue
⊙	931			0921	dk blue
X	932			0920	blue
8	3041			0872	lavender
V	3042			0870	lt lavender
3	3045	◣		0888	dk yellow beige
−	3046	◣		0887	yellow beige
◈	3047	◣	◩	0852	lt yellow beige
6	3325	▢		0129	lt blue
C	3328	◣		010	rose
5	3364	◣		0265	olive green
⊙	781			0309	gold Fr. Knot

▢ Grey area indicates last row of left side of design

† Dk grey brown for window frame only. Gold for all other.

★ Beige grey for shadows on window only. Vy dk blue for all other.

* Dk golden brown for hat only. Vy dk brown for all other.

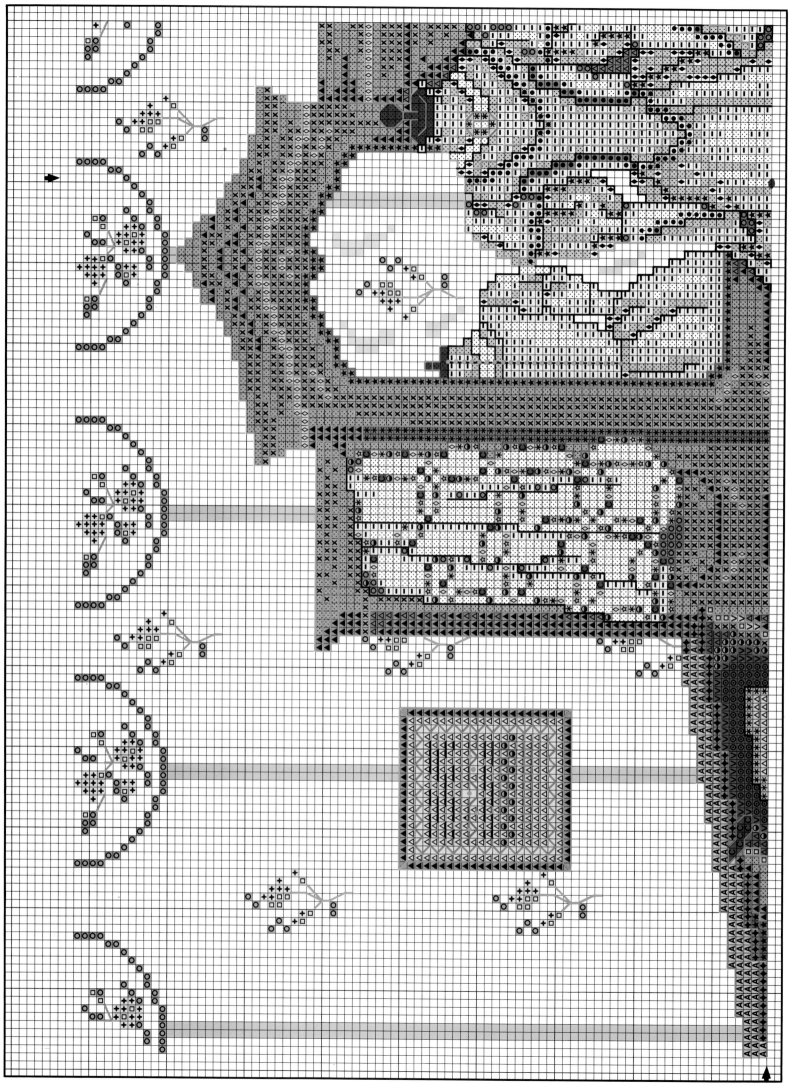

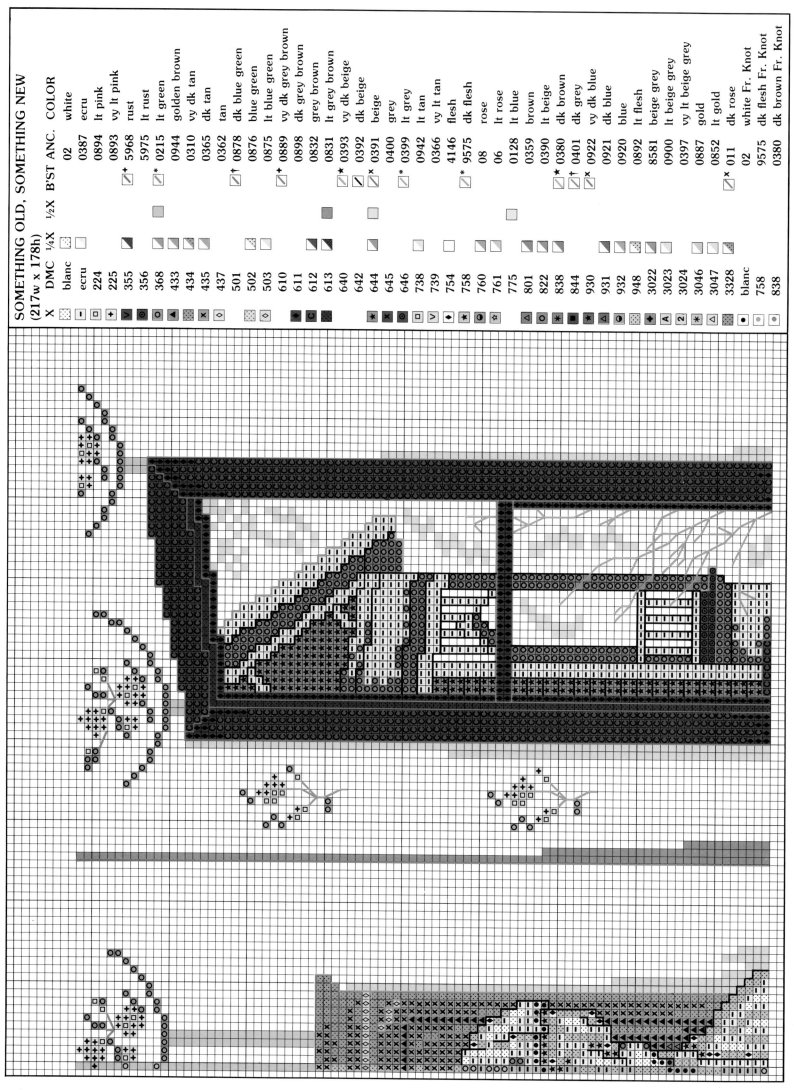

X	DMC	ANC.	B'ST	¼X	½X	COLOR
	blanc	02				white
	ecru	0387				ecru
	224	0894				lt pink
	225	0893				vy lt pink
	355	5968	+			rust
	356	5975	*			lt rust
	368	0215				lt green
	433	0944				golden brown
	434	0310				vy dk tan
	435	0365				dk tan
	437	0362				tan
	501	0878	†			dk blue green
	502	0876				blue green
	503	0875	+			lt blue green
	610	0889				vy dk grey brown
	611	0898				dk grey brown
	612	0832				grey brown
	613	0831				lt grey brown
	640	0393	★			vy dk beige
	642	0392				dk beige
	644	0391	×			beige
	645	0400				grey
	646	0399	*			lt grey
	738	0942				lt tan
	739	0366				vy lt tan
	754	4146				flesh
	758	9575	*			dk flesh
	760	08				rose
	761	06				lt rose
	775	0128				lt blue
	801	0359				brown
	822	0390				lt beige
	838	0380	★			dk brown
	844	0401	†			dk grey
	930	0922	×			vy dk blue
	931	0921				dk blue
	932	0920				blue
	948	0892				lt flesh
	3022	8581				beige grey
	3023	0900				lt beige grey
	3024	0397				vy lt beige grey
	3046	0887				gold
	3047	0852				lt gold
	3328	011	×			dk rose
	blanc	02				white Fr. Knot
	758	9575				dk flesh Fr. Knot
	838	0380				dk brown Fr. Knot

104

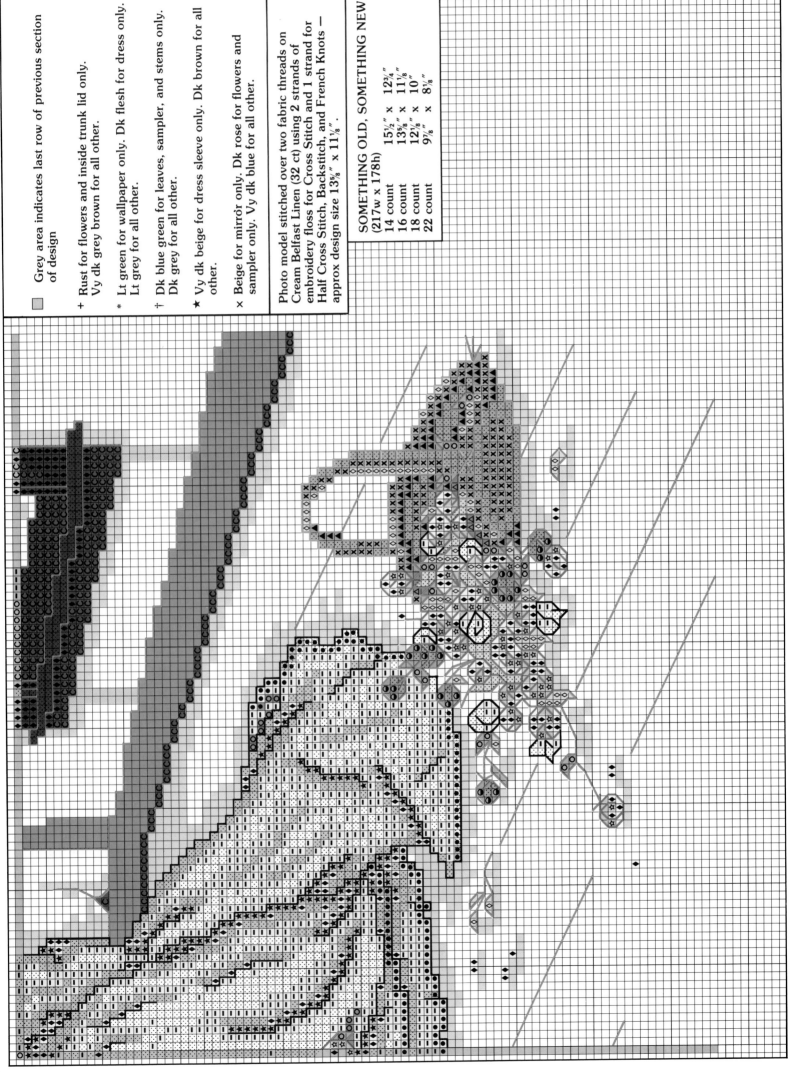

■ Grey area indicates last row of previous section of design

+ Rust for flowers and inside trunk lid only. Vy dk grey brown for all other.

* Lt green for wallpaper only. Dk flesh for dress only. Lt grey for all other.

† Dk blue green for leaves, sampler, and stems only. Dk grey for all other.

★ Vy dk beige for dress sleeve only. Dk brown for all other.

× Beige for mirror only. Dk rose for flowers and sampler only. Vy dk blue for all other.

Photo model stitched over two fabric threads on Cream Belfast Linen (32 ct) using 2 strands of embroidery floss for Cross Stitch and 1 strand for Half Cross Stitch, Backstitch, and French Knots — approx design size 13⅝" x 11⅛".

SOMETHING OLD, SOMETHING NEW (217w x 178h)

14 count	15½"	x	12¾"
16 count	13⅝"	x	11⅛"
18 count	12⅛"	x	10"
22 count	9⅞"	x	8⅛"

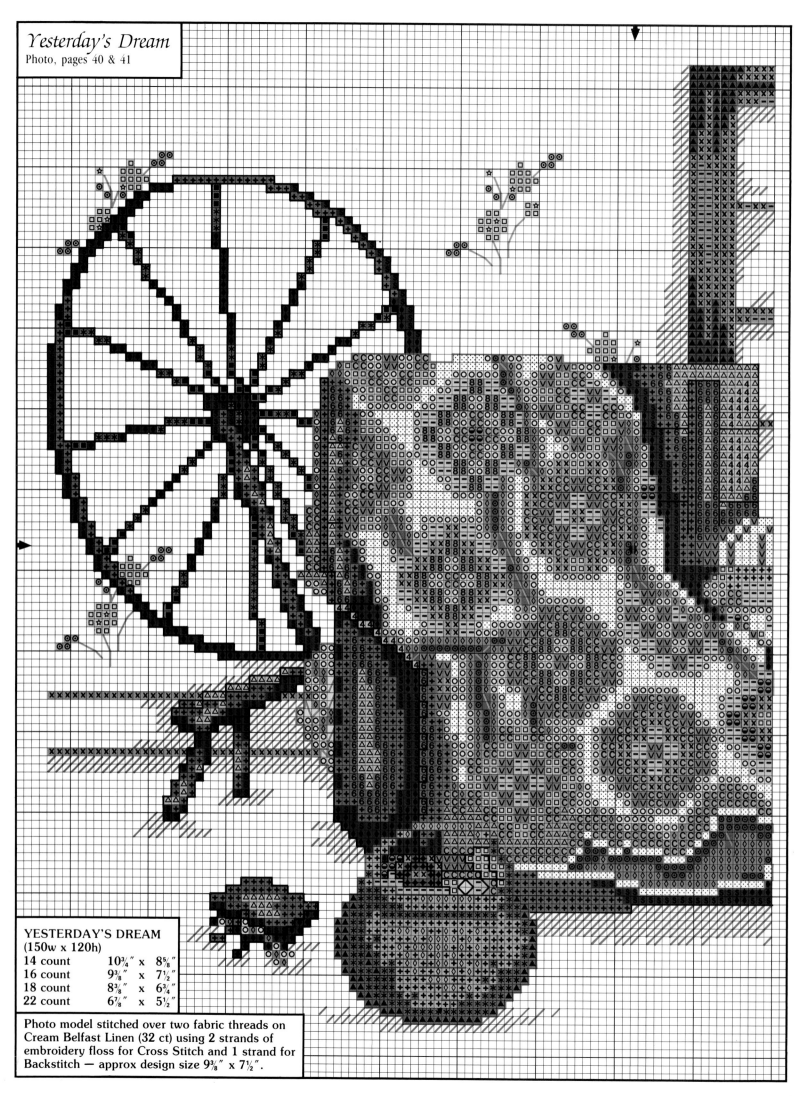

Yesterday's Dream
Photo, pages 40 & 41

YESTERDAY'S DREAM
(150w x 120h)

14 count	10¾"	x 8⅝"
16 count	9⅜"	x 7½"
18 count	8⅜"	x 6¾"
22 count	6⅞"	x 5½"

Photo model stitched over two fabric threads on Cream Belfast Linen (32 ct) using 2 strands of embroidery floss for Cross Stitch and 1 strand for Backstitch — approx design size 9⅜" x 7½".

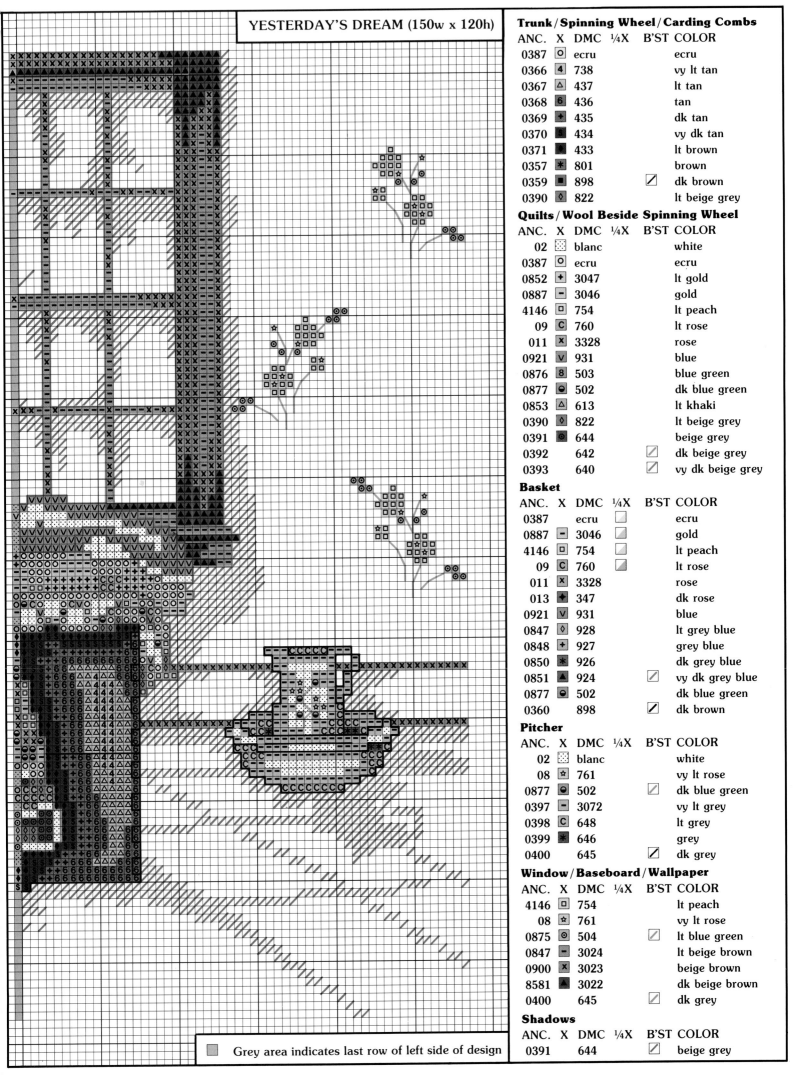

YESTERDAY'S DREAM (150w x 120h)

Trunk / Spinning Wheel / Carding Combs

ANC.	X	DMC	¼X	B'ST	COLOR
0387	○	ecru			ecru
0366	4	738			vy lt tan
0367	△	437			lt tan
0368	6	436			tan
0369	✦	435			dk tan
0370	◪	434			vy dk tan
0371	◼	433			lt brown
0357	✳	801			brown
0359	◼	898		╱	dk brown
0390	◇	822			lt beige grey

Quilts / Wool Beside Spinning Wheel

ANC.	X	DMC	¼X	B'ST	COLOR
02	⬚	blanc			white
0387	○	ecru			ecru
0852	+	3047			lt gold
0887	−	3046			gold
4146	☐	754			lt peach
09	C	760			lt rose
011	X	3328			rose
0921	V	931			blue
0876	8	503			blue green
0877	◉	502			dk blue green
0853	△	613			lt khaki
0390	◇	822			lt beige grey
0391	◉	644			beige grey
0392		642		╱	dk beige grey
0393		640		╱	vy dk beige grey

Basket

ANC.	X	DMC	¼X	B'ST	COLOR
0387		ecru	◻		ecru
0887	−	3046	◸		gold
4146	☐	754	◸		lt peach
09	C	760	◸		lt rose
011	X	3328			rose
013	✦	347			dk rose
0921	V	931			blue
0847	◇	928			lt grey blue
0848	+	927			grey blue
0850	✳	926			dk grey blue
0851	▲	924		╱	vy dk grey blue
0877	◉	502			dk blue green
0360		898		╱	dk brown

Pitcher

ANC.	X	DMC	¼X	B'ST	COLOR
02	⬚	blanc			white
08	☆	761			vy lt rose
0877	◉	502		╱	dk blue green
0397	−	3072			vy lt grey
0398	C	648			lt grey
0399	✳	646			grey
0400		645		╱	dk grey

Window / Baseboard / Wallpaper

ANC.	X	DMC	¼X	B'ST	COLOR
4146	☐	754			lt peach
08	☆	761			vy lt rose
0875	◉	504		╱	lt blue green
0847	−	3024			lt beige brown
0900	X	3023			beige brown
8581	▲	3022			dk beige brown
0400		645		╱	dk grey

Shadows

ANC.	X	DMC	¼X	B'ST	COLOR
0391		644		╱	beige grey

⬚ Grey area indicates last row of left side of design

Photo model stitched over two fabric threads on Cream Belfast Linen (32 ct) using 2 strands of embroidery floss for Cross Stitch and

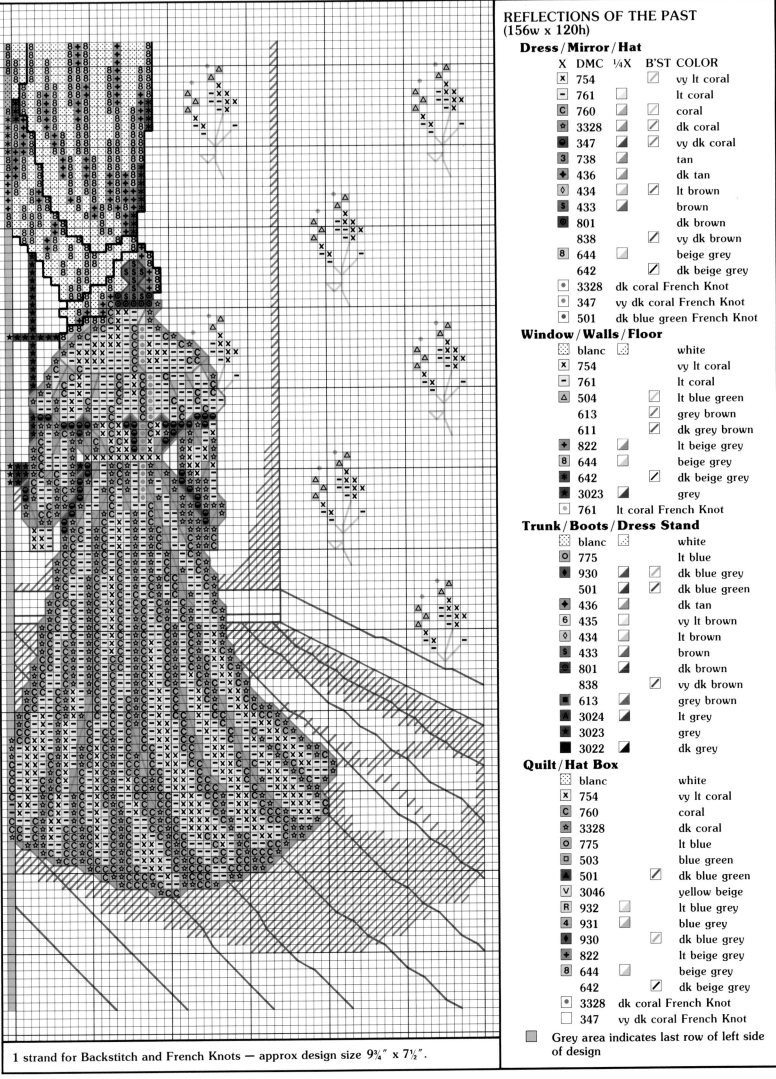

REFLECTIONS OF THE PAST
(156w x 120h)

Dress / Mirror / Hat

X	DMC	¼X	B'ST	COLOR
x	754		⊘	vy lt coral
-	761	◪		lt coral
C	760	◪	⊘	coral
☆	3328	◪	⊘	dk coral
◉	347	◪	⊘	vy dk coral
3	738	◪		tan
✦	436	◪		dk tan
◇	434		⊘	lt brown
S	433	◪		brown
◉	801	◪		dk brown
	838		⊘	vy dk brown
8	644	◪		beige grey
	642		⊘	dk beige grey
⊙	3328			dk coral French Knot
⊙	347			vy dk coral French Knot
⊙	501			dk blue green French Knot

Window / Walls / Floor

X	DMC	¼X	B'ST	COLOR
⊡	blanc	⊡		white
x	754			vy lt coral
-	761			lt coral
△	504		⊘	lt blue green
	613		⊘	grey brown
	611		⊘	dk grey brown
✦	822	◪		lt beige grey
8	644	◪		beige grey
✳	642		⊘	dk beige grey
✳	3023	◪		grey
⊙	761			lt coral French Knot

Trunk / Boots / Dress Stand

X	DMC	¼X	B'ST	COLOR
⊡	blanc	⊡		white
O	775			lt blue
◆	930	◪	⊘	dk blue grey
	501	◪	⊘	dk blue green
✦	436	◪		dk tan
6	435	◪		vy lt brown
◇	434	◪		lt brown
S	433	◪		brown
◙	801	◪		dk brown
	838		⊘	vy dk brown
■	613	◪		grey brown
A	3024	◪		lt grey
★	3023			grey
■	3022	◪		dk grey

Quilt / Hat Box

X	DMC	¼X	B'ST	COLOR
⊡	blanc	⊡		white
x	754			vy lt coral
C	760			coral
☆	3328			dk coral
O	775			lt blue
☐	503			blue green
▲	501		⊘	dk blue green
V	3046			yellow beige
R	932	◪		lt blue grey
4	931	◪		blue grey
◆	930		⊘	dk blue grey
✦	822			lt beige grey
8	644	◪		beige grey
	642		⊘	dk beige grey
⊙	3328			dk coral French Knot
☐	347			vy dk coral French Knot

⬛ Grey area indicates last row of left side of design

1 strand for Backstitch and French Knots — approx design size 9¾" x 7½".

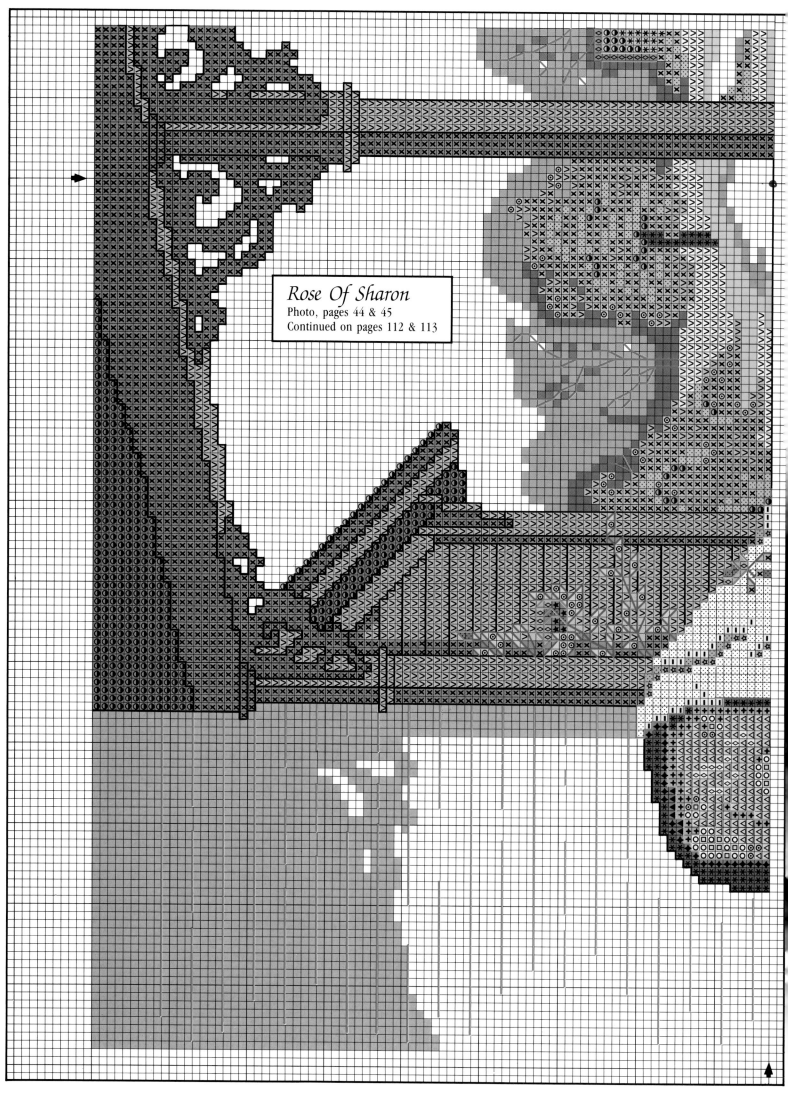

Rose Of Sharon
Photo, pages 44 & 45
Continued on pages 112 & 113

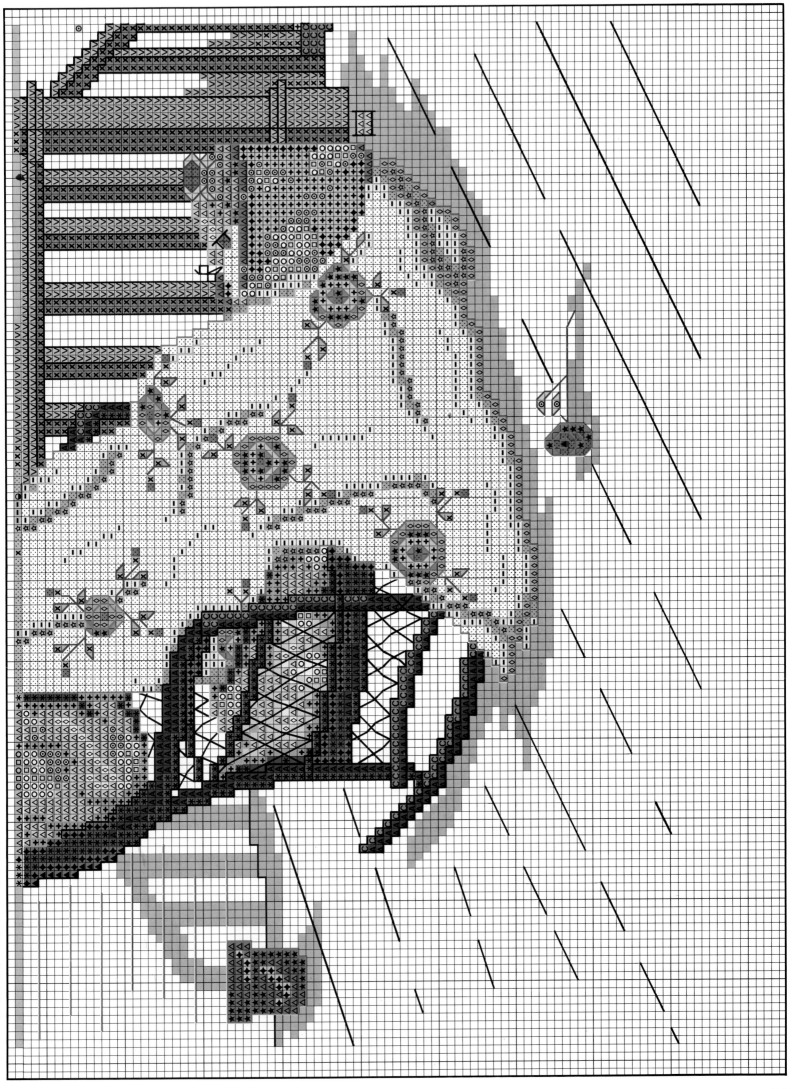

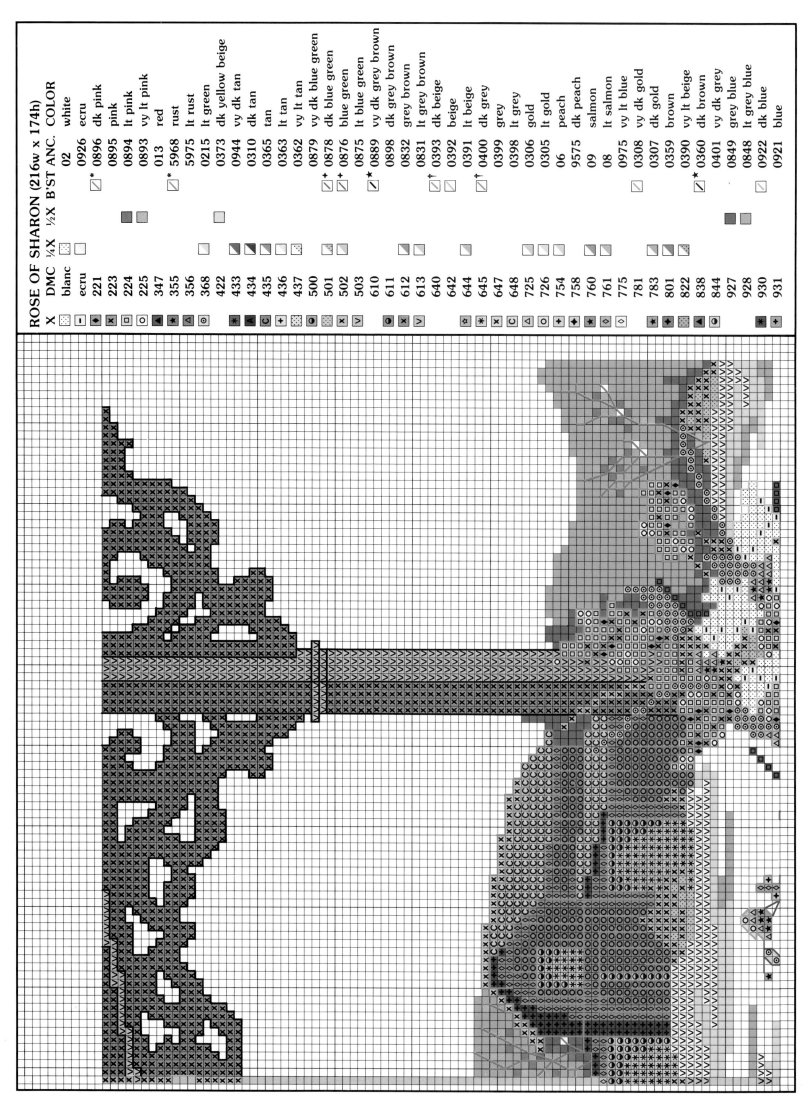

ROSE OF SHARON (216w x 174h)

X	¼X	½X	B'ST	DMC	ANC.	COLOR
				blanc	02	white
				ecru	0926	ecru
				221	0896	dk pink
			*	223	0895	pink
				224	0894	lt pink
				225	0893	vy lt pink
				347	013	red
				355	5968	rust
			*	356	5975	lt rust
				368	0215	lt green
				422	0373	dk yellow beige
				433	0944	vy dk tan
				434	0310	dk tan
				435	0365	tan
				436	0363	lt tan
				437	0362	vy lt tan
				500	0879	vy dk blue green
			+	501	0878	dk blue green
				502	0876	blue green
				503	0875	lt blue green
				610	0889	vy dk grey brown
			★	611	0898	dk grey brown
				612	0832	grey brown
				613	0831	lt grey brown
				640	0393	dk beige
			†	642	0392	beige
				644	0391	lt beige
				645	0400	dk grey
			†	647	0399	grey
				648	0398	lt grey
				725	0306	gold
				726	0305	lt gold
				754	06	peach
				758	9575	dk peach
				760	09	salmon
				761	08	lt salmon
				775	0975	vy lt blue
				781	0308	vy dk gold
				783	0307	dk gold
				801	0359	brown
				822	0390	vy lt beige
			★	838	0360	dk brown
				844	0401	vy dk grey
				927	0849	grey blue
				928	0848	lt grey blue
				930	0922	dk blue
				931	0921	blue

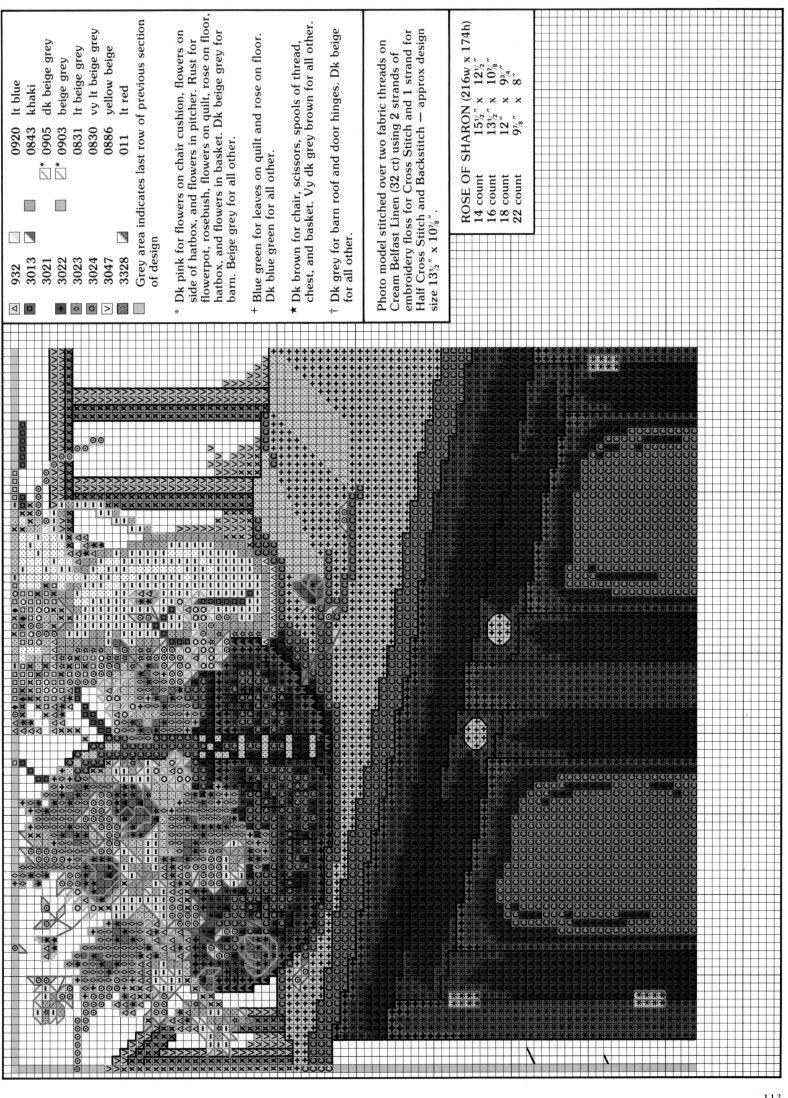

932	0920	lt blue
3013	0843	khaki
3021	0905 *	dk beige grey
3022	0903 *	beige grey
3023	0831	lt beige grey
3024	0830	vy lt beige grey
3047	0886	yellow beige
3328	011	lt red

Grey area indicates last row of previous section of design

* Dk pink for flowers on chair cushion, flowers on side of hatbox, and flowers in pitcher. Rust for flowerpot, rosebush, flowers on quilt, rose on floor, hatbox, and flowers in basket. Dk beige grey for barn. Beige grey for all other.

+ Blue green for leaves on quilt and rose on floor. Dk blue green for all other.

★ Dk brown for chair, scissors, spools of thread, chest, and basket. Vy dk grey brown for all other.

† Dk grey for barn roof and door hinges. Dk beige for all other.

Photo model stitched over two fabric threads on Cream Belfast Linen (32 ct) using 2 strands of embroidery floss for Cross Stitch and 1 strand for Half Cross Stitch and Backstitch — approx design size 13½" x 10⅛".

ROSE OF SHARON (216w x 174h)

14 count	15½"	x	12½"
16 count	13½"	x	10⅞"
18 count	12"	x	9¾"
22 count	9⅞"	x	8"

Photo model stitched over two fabric threads on Cream Belfast Linen (32 ct) using **2** strands of embroidery floss for Cross Stitch and

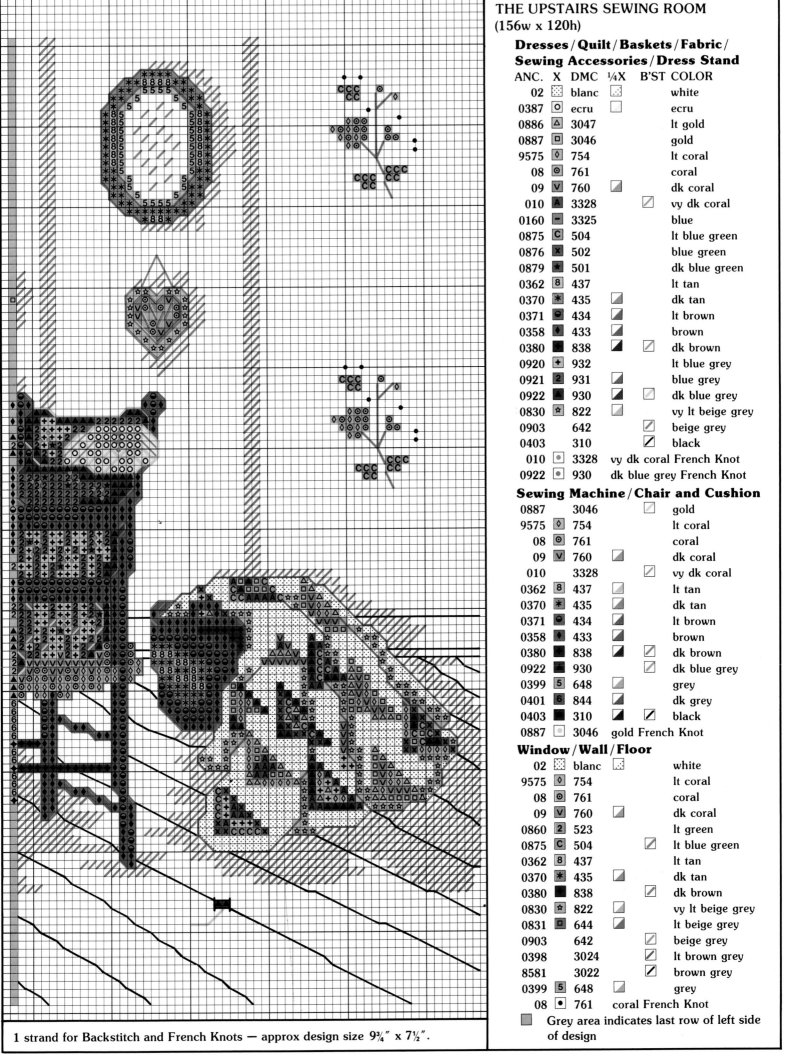

THE UPSTAIRS SEWING ROOM
(156w x 120h)

Dresses / Quilt / Baskets / Fabric / Sewing Accessories / Dress Stand

ANC.	X	DMC	¼X	B'ST	COLOR
02	▨	blanc	▨		white
0387	⊙	ecru	☐		ecru
0886	△	3047			lt gold
0887	☐	3046			gold
9575	◇	754			lt coral
08	⊙	761			coral
09	V	760	◩		dk coral
010	▲	3328		◲	vy dk coral
0160	−	3325			blue
0875	C	504			lt blue green
0876	✕	502			blue green
0879	★	501			dk blue green
0362	8	437			lt tan
0370	*	435	◩		dk tan
0371	◉	434	◩		lt brown
0358	◆	433	◩		brown
0380	■	838	◩	◲	dk brown
0920	+	932			lt blue grey
0921	2	931	◩		blue grey
0922	▲	930	◩		dk blue grey
0830	☆	822	◩		vy lt beige grey
0903		642		◲	beige grey
0403		310		◲	black
010	⊙	3328			vy dk coral French Knot
0922	⊙	930			dk blue grey French Knot

Sewing Machine / Chair and Cushion

ANC.	X	DMC	¼X	B'ST	COLOR
0887		3046		◲	gold
9575	◇	754			lt coral
08	⊙	761			coral
09	V	760	◩		dk coral
010		3328		◲	vy dk coral
0362	8	437	◩		lt tan
0370	*	435	◩		dk tan
0371	◉	434	◩		lt brown
0358	◆	433	◩		brown
0380	■	838	◩	◲	dk brown
0922	■	930	◩	◲	dk blue grey
0399	5	648	◩		grey
0401	6	844	◩	◲	dk grey
0403	■	310	◩	◲	black
0887	⊙	3046			gold French Knot

Window / Wall / Floor

ANC.	X	DMC	¼X	B'ST	COLOR
02	▨	blanc	▨		white
9575	◇	754			lt coral
08	⊙	761			coral
09	V	760	◩		dk coral
0860	2	523			lt green
0875	C	504		◲	lt blue green
0362	8	437			lt tan
0370	*	435	◩		dk tan
0380	■	838		◲	dk brown
0830	☆	822			vy lt beige grey
0831	☐	644	◩		lt beige grey
0903		642		◲	beige grey
0398		3024		◲	lt brown grey
8581		3022		◲	brown grey
0399	5	648	◩		grey
08	⊙	761			coral French Knot

▨ Grey area indicates last row of left side of design

1 strand for Backstitch and French Knots — approx design size 9¾" x 7½".

115

Photo model stitched over two fabric
threads on Cream Belfast Linen
(32 ct) using 2 strands of embroidery
floss for Cross Stitch and 1 strand
for Backstitch and French Knot —
approx design size 6⅜" x 6⅝".

PINK RIBBON (102w x 106h)
14 count	7⅜"	x 7⅝"
16 count	6⅜"	x 6⅝"
18 count	5¾"	x 6"
22 count	4¾"	x 4⅞"

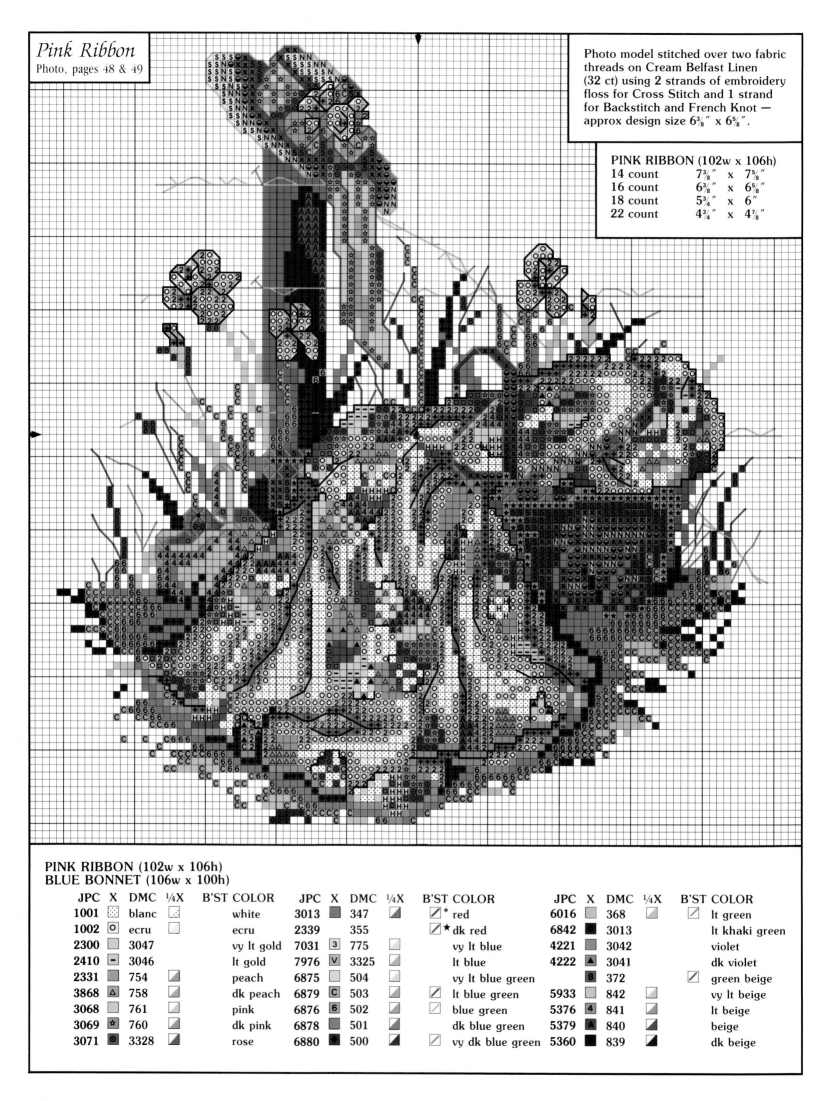

PINK RIBBON (102w x 106h)
BLUE BONNET (106w x 100h)

JPC	X	DMC	¼X	B'ST	COLOR	JPC	X	DMC	¼X	B'ST	COLOR	JPC	X	DMC	¼X	B'ST	COLOR
1001		blanc			white	3013		347		◪*	red	6016		368			lt green
1002	○	ecru			ecru	2339		355		◪★	dk red	6842		3013			lt khaki green
2300		3047			vy lt gold	7031	3	775			vy lt blue	4221		3042			violet
2410	-	3046			lt gold	7976	V	3325			lt blue	4222	▲	3041			dk violet
2331		754			peach	6875		504			vy lt blue green		8	372		◪	green beige
3868	△	758			dk peach	6879	C	503		◪	lt blue green	5933		842			vy lt beige
3068		761			pink	6876	6	502			blue green	5376	4	841			lt beige
3069	★	760			dk pink	6878		501			dk blue green	5379	▲	840			beige
3071	◉	3328			rose	6880	✦	500		◪	vy dk blue green	5360		839		◪	dk beige

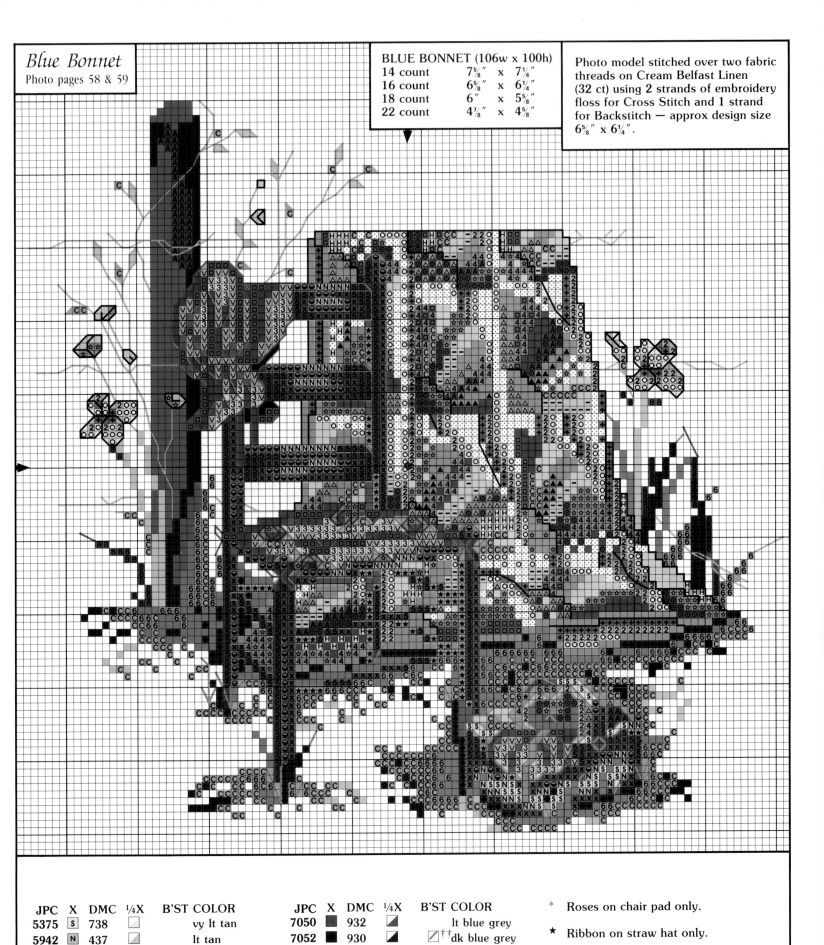

Blue Bonnet
Photo pages 58 & 59

BLUE BONNET (106w x 100h)

14 count	7⅝" x 7¼"
16 count	6⅝" x 6¼"
18 count	6" x 5⅝"
22 count	4⅞" x 4⅝"

Photo model stitched over two fabric threads on Cream Belfast Linen (32 ct) using 2 strands of embroidery floss for Cross Stitch and 1 strand for Backstitch — approx design size 6⅝" x 6¼".

JPC	X	DMC	¼X	B'ST	COLOR
5375	s	738			vy lt tan
5942	N	437			lt tan
5371	⊙	435			tan
5000	✕	434			dk tan
5471	5	433	⊘**		vy dk tan
5475	★	801			brown
5381		838	⊘†		dk brown
7225	H	928			vy lt blue grey
7051	▣	931			blue grey

JPC	X	DMC	¼X	B'ST	COLOR
7050		932			lt blue grey
7052		930		⊘††	dk blue grey
5830	2	822			vy lt grey
5831	+	644			lt grey
5832		642		⊘	grey
5381	•	838			dk brown French Knot

* Roses on chair pad only.

★ Ribbon on straw hat only.

** Barbed wire and straw hat only.

† Nails, pincushions, hoop, baskets, and chair only.

†† Blue bonnet, chair pad, and blue fabric only.

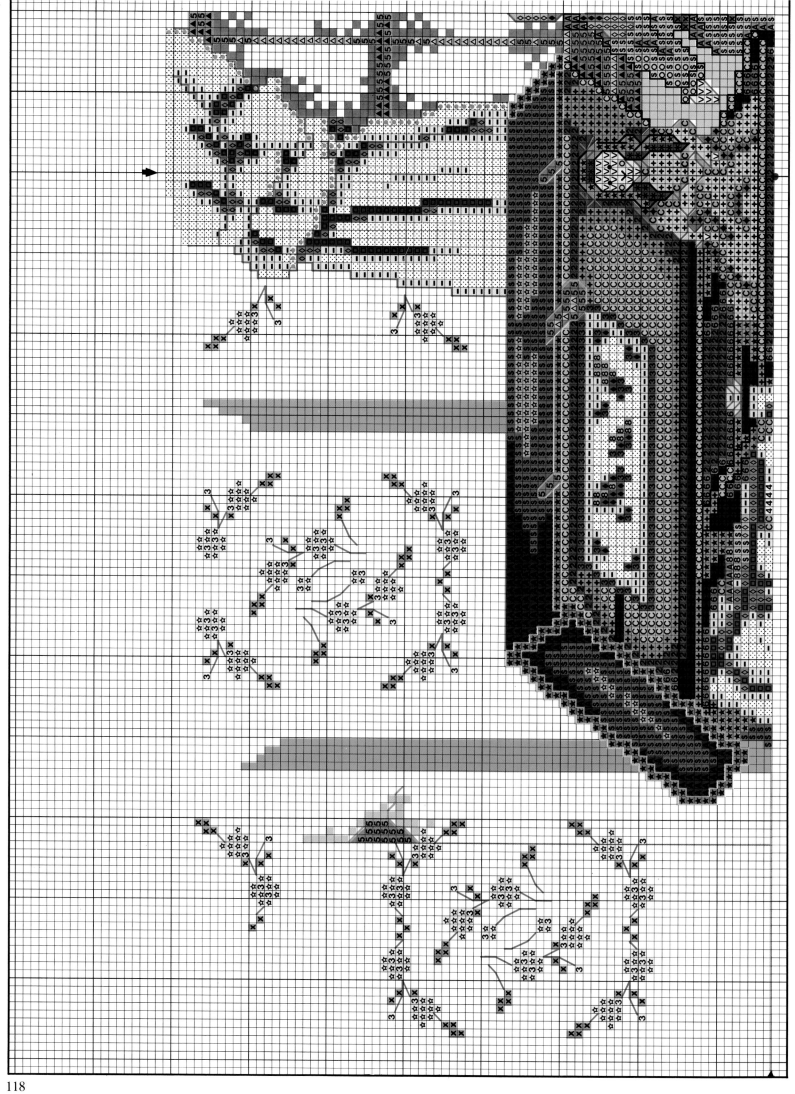

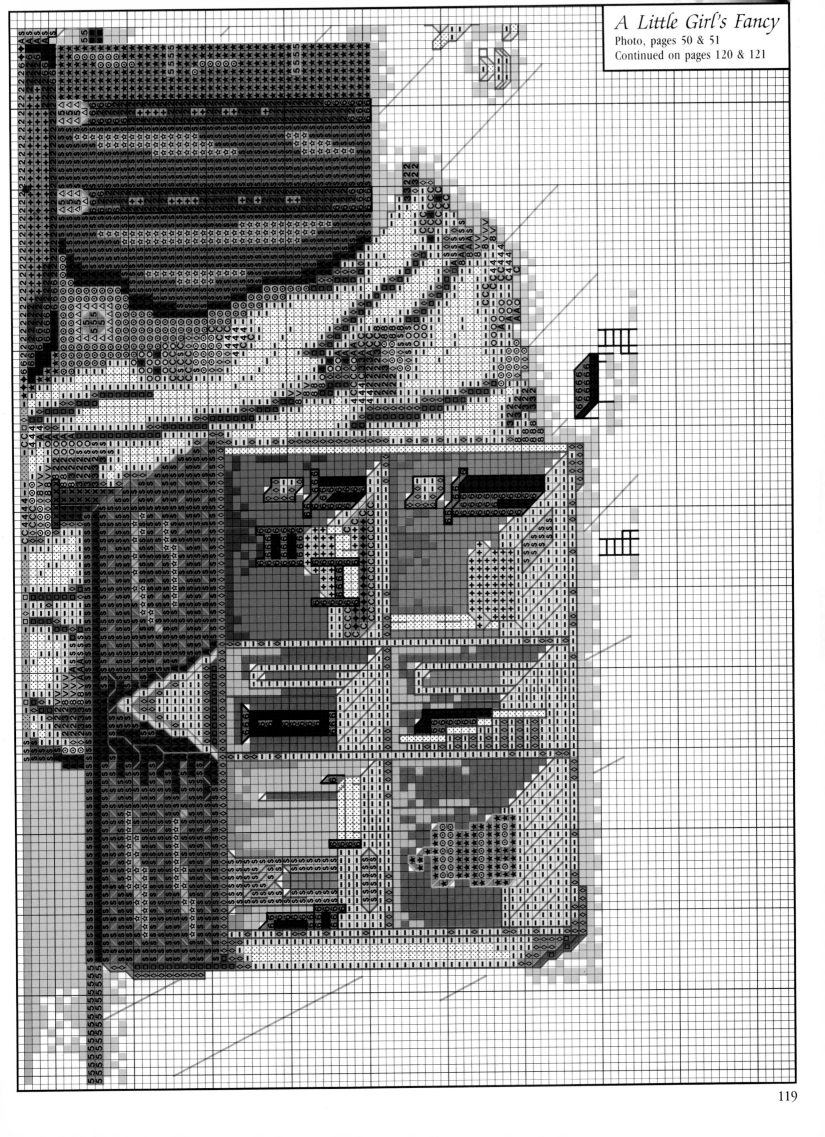

A LITTLE GIRL'S FANCY (222w x 156h)

X	¼X	½X	B'ST	ANC.	DMC	COLOR
				02	blanc	white
				0387	ecru	ecru
				0893	224	pink
				0894	225	lt pink
				0403	310	black
				013	347	vy dk rose
			+	5968	355	rust
			*	0214	368	green
			†	0906	420	vy dk gold
				0887	422	gold
				0310	434	vy dk tan
			†	0365	435	dk tan
				0362	437	tan
				0877	502	dk blue green
				0876	503	blue green
				0875	504	lt blue green
				0889	611	dk beige
				0898	612	beige
				0831	613	lt beige
				0393	640	dk grey beige
			*	0392	642	grey beige
				0388	644	lt grey beige
				0400	645	grey
				0361	738	lt tan
				0366	739	vy lt tan
				4146	754	flesh
				09	760	rose
				08	761	lt rose
				0128	775	vy lt blue
			★	0359	801	golden brown
				0390	822	vy lt grey beige
			+	0380	838	brown
				0401	844	dk grey
			†	0922	930	vy dk blue
				0921	931	dk blue
				0920	932	blue
				0892	948	lt flesh
			★	0401	3021	dk brown grey
				0399	3022	brown grey
				0398	3023	lt brown grey
				0397	3024	vy lt brown grey
				0872	3041	lavender
				0870	3042	lt lavender
				0888	3045	dk gold
				0886	3046	lt gold
				0852	3047	vy lt gold
				0129	3325	lt blue
			+	011	3328	dk rose

A LITTLE GIRL'S FANCY (222w x 156h)

14 count	15⅞"	x	11¼"
16 count	13⅞"	x	9¾"
18 count	12⅜"	x	8¾"
22 count	10⅛"	x	7⅛"

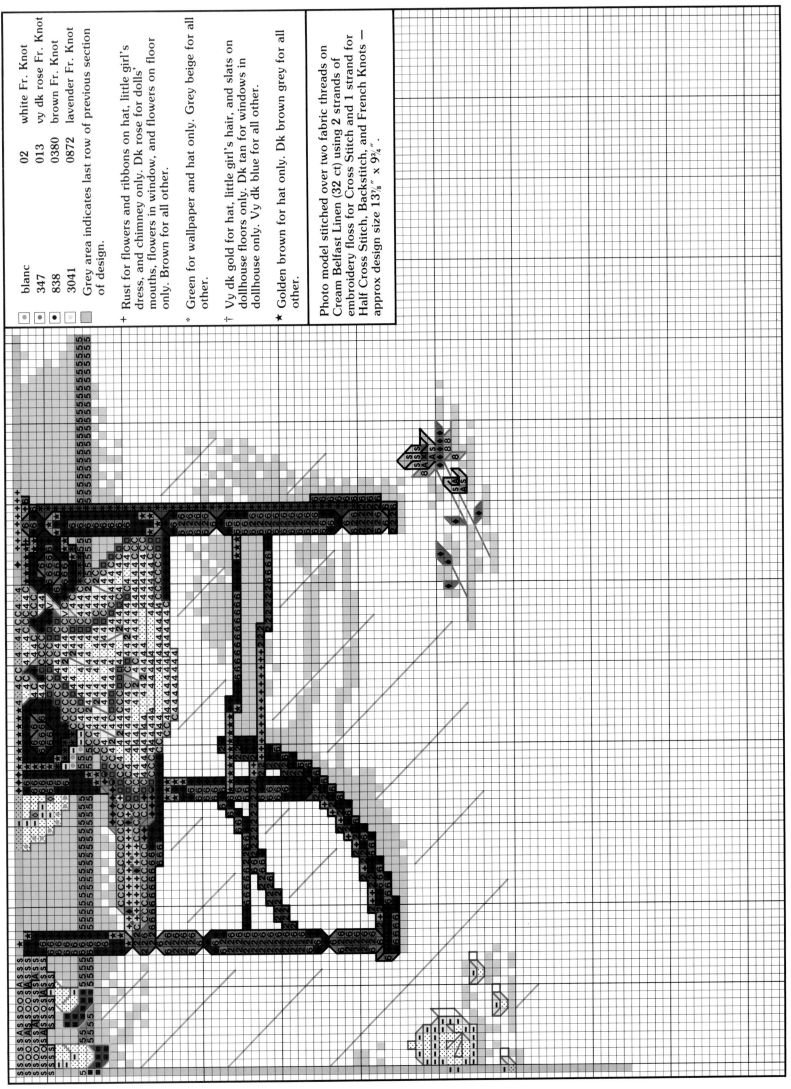

blanc
347
838
3041

02   white Fr. Knot
013   vy dk rose Fr. Knot
0380   brown Fr. Knot
0872   lavender Fr. Knot

Grey area indicates last row of previous section of design.

+ Rust for flowers and ribbons on hat, little girl's dress, and chimney only. Dk rose for dolls' mouths, flowers in window, and flowers on floor only. Brown for all other.

* Green for wallpaper and hat only. Grey beige for all other.

† Vy dk gold for hat, little girl's hair, and slats on dollhouse floors only. Dk tan for windows in dollhouse only. Vy dk blue for all other.

★ Golden brown for hat only. Dk brown grey for all other.

Photo model stitched over two fabric threads on Cream Belfast Linen (32 ct) using 2 strands of embroidery floss for Cross Stitch and 1 strand for Half Cross Stitch, Backstitch, and French Knots — approx design size 13⅞" x 9¾".

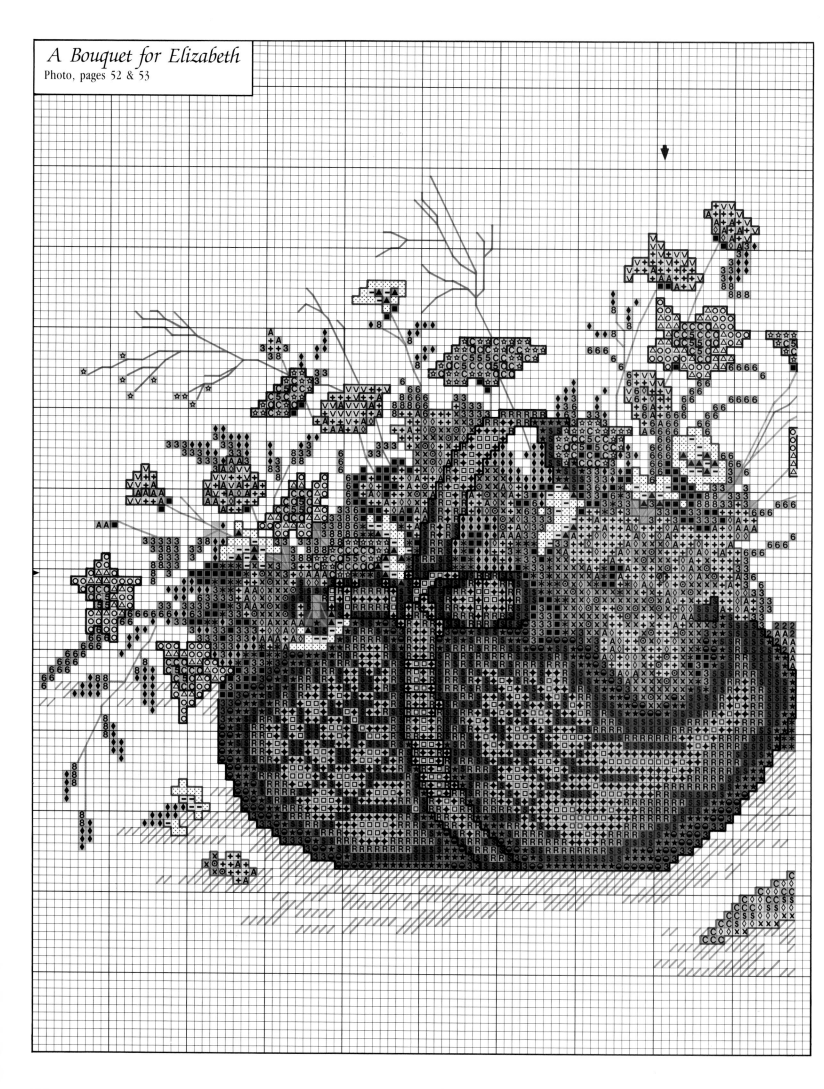

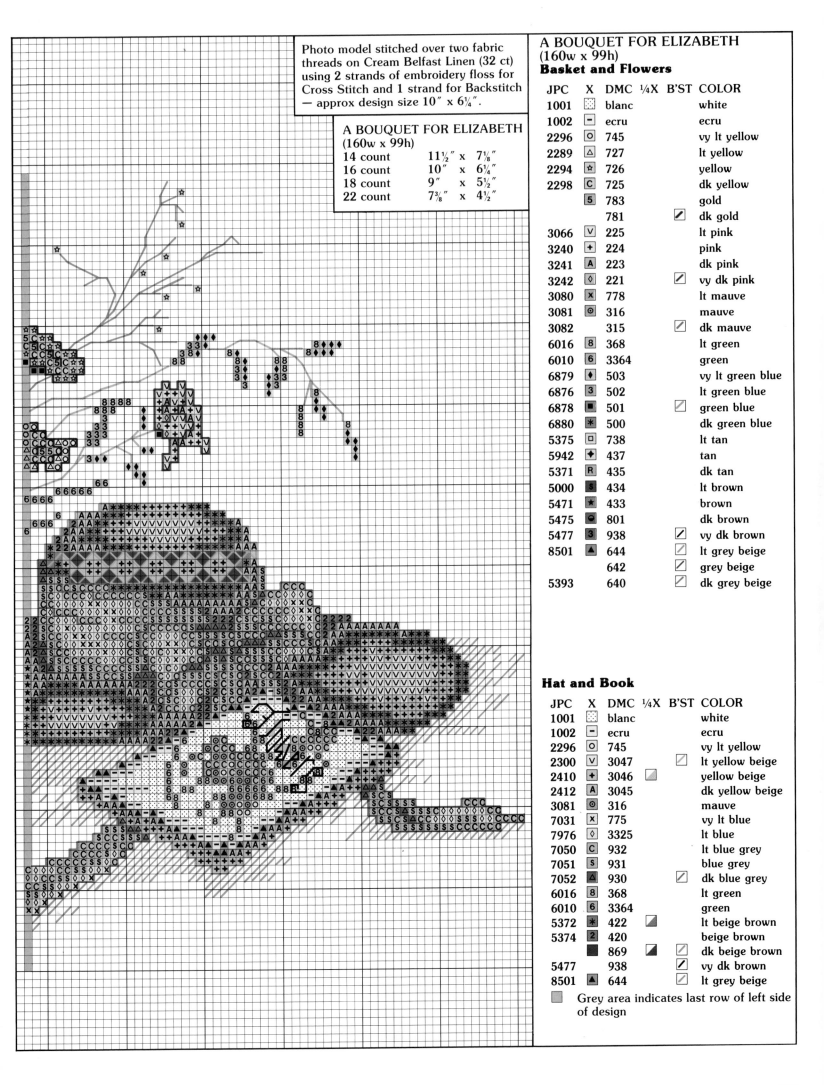

Photo model stitched over two fabric threads on Cream Belfast Linen (32 ct) using 2 strands of embroidery floss for Cross Stitch and 1 strand for Backstitch — approx design size 10″ x 6¼″.

A BOUQUET FOR ELIZABETH
(160w x 99h)

14 count	11½″ x	7⅛″
16 count	10″ x	6¼″
18 count	9″ x	5½″
22 count	7⅜″ x	4½″

A BOUQUET FOR ELIZABETH
(160w x 99h)
Basket and Flowers

JPC	X	DMC	¼X	B'ST	COLOR
1001	⊡	blanc			white
1002	–	ecru			ecru
2296	O	745			vy lt yellow
2289	△	727			lt yellow
2294	☆	726			yellow
2298	C	725			dk yellow
	5	783			gold
		781		✓	dk gold
3066	V	225			lt pink
3240	+	224			pink
3241	A	223			dk pink
3242	◇	221		✓	vy dk pink
3080	✗	778			lt mauve
3081	⊙	316			mauve
3082		315		✓	dk mauve
6016	8	368			lt green
6010	6	3364			green
6879	◆	503			vy lt green blue
6876	3	502			lt green blue
6878	■	501		✓	green blue
6880	✳	500			dk green blue
5375	▫	738			lt tan
5942	◆	437			tan
5371	R	435			dk tan
5000	S	434			lt brown
5471	★	433			brown
5475	◓	801			dk brown
5477	3	938		✓	vy dk brown
8501	▲	644		✓	lt grey beige
		642		✓	grey beige
5393		640		✓	dk grey beige

Hat and Book

JPC	X	DMC	¼X	B'ST	COLOR
1001	⊡	blanc			white
1002	–	ecru			ecru
2296	O	745			vy lt yellow
2300	V	3047		✓	lt yellow beige
2410	+	3046	◩		yellow beige
2412	A	3045			dk yellow beige
3081	⊙	316			mauve
7031	✗	775			vy lt blue
7976	◇	3325			lt blue
7050	C	932			lt blue grey
7051	S	931			blue grey
7052	△	930		✓	dk blue grey
6016	8	368			lt green
6010	6	3364			green
5372	✳	422	◩		lt beige brown
5374	2	420			beige brown
	■	869	◩	✓	dk beige brown
5477		938		✓	vy dk brown
8501	▲	644		✓	lt grey beige

Grey area indicates last row of left side of design

123

THE SEAMSTRESS (128w x 137h)

X	DMC	¼X	B'ST	JPC	COLOR
░	blanc	░		1001	white
-	ecru	☐		1002	ecru
☒	224			3240	pink
◊	225			3066	lt pink
	310		◪*	8403	black
✶	347	◪		3013	red
+	355		◪†	2339	rust
V	356	◪		2975	lt rust
A	368	◪	◪*	6016	green
✶	433			5471	vy dk tan
☒	434	◪		5000	dk tan
◊	435	◪		5371	tan
▦	437	◪		5942	lt tan
✱	501	◪	◪*	6878	dk blue green
░	502	░		6876	blue green
◉	554			4104	violet
A	611		◪★	5898	dk grey brown
V	612	◪	◪†		grey brown
◉	613		◪+		lt grey brown
	640	◪		5393	dk beige
C	642	◪		5832	beige
☆	644	◪	◪☆	5831	lt beige
▲	645			8500	dk grey
☒	647	░		8900	grey
	726		◪+	2295	gold
▦	754			3146	peach
◆	758			3868	dk peach
▦	760	◪		3069	salmon
▢	761	◪		3068	lt salmon
	775		◪×	7031	lt blue
✶	801	◪		5475	brown
◉	822			5830	vy lt beige
■	838		◪×	5831	dk brown
✶	844	◪		8501	vy dk grey
☒	931		◪★	7051	blue
◉	948			2331	lt peach
▲	3328		◪☆	3071	lt red
●	347			3013	red Fr. Knot

☐ Blue area indicates first row of right section of design.

* Black for sewing machine. Green for wallpaper flower stems. Dk blue green for all other.

† Grey brown for seam in wallpaper. Rust for all other.

★ Blue for spool of thread and ribbon in drawer. Dk grey brown for all other.

+ Gold for trim on sewing machine. Lt grey brown for all other.

☆ Lt beige for shading. Lt red for all other.

× Lt blue for shading. Dk brown for all other.

Photo model stitched over two fabric threads on Cream Belfast Linen (32 ct) using 2 strands of embroidery floss for Cross Stitch and 1 strand for Backstitch and French Knots — approx design size 8″ x 8⅝″.

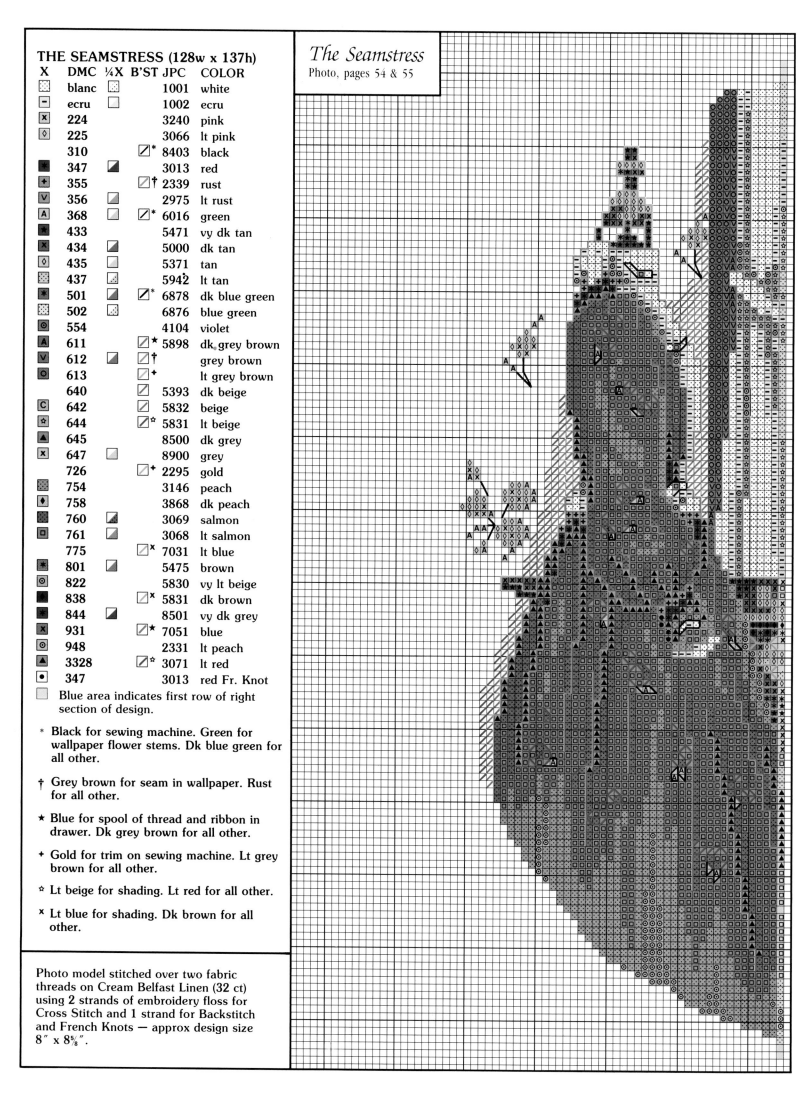

THE SEAMSTRESS (128w x 137h)

count	width		height
14 count	9¼″	x	9⅞″
16 count	8″	. x	8⅝″
18 count	7⅛″	x	7⅝″
22 count	5⅞″	x	6¼″

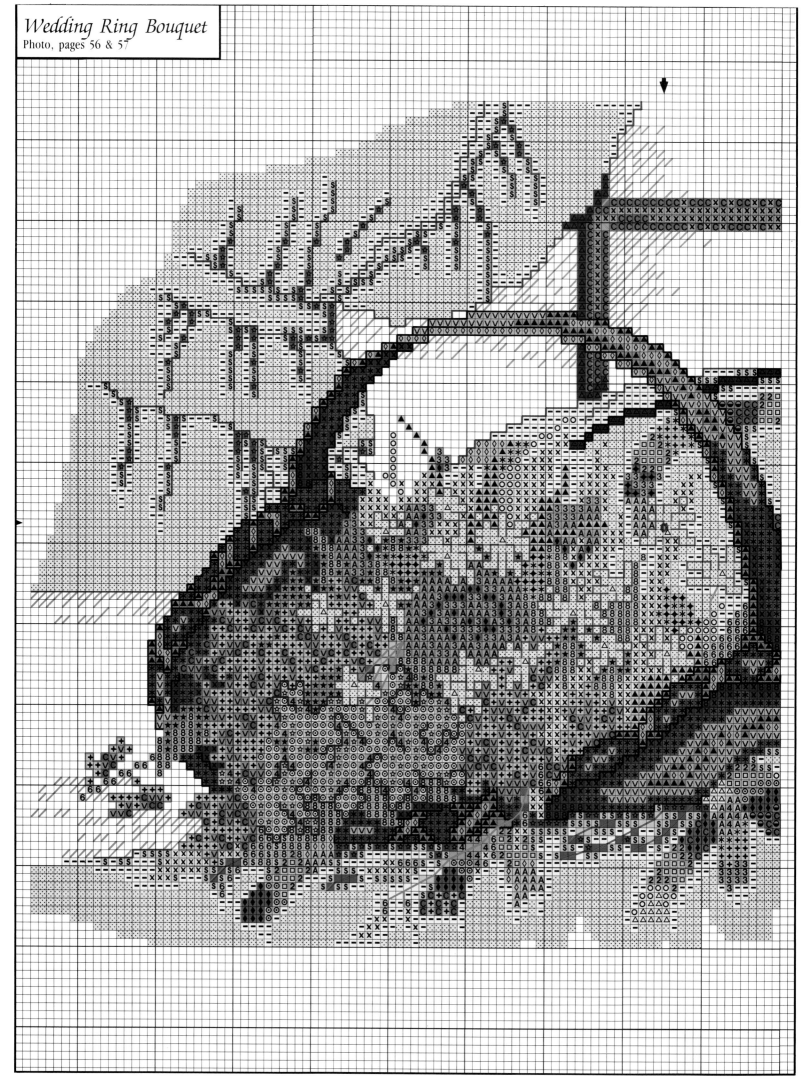

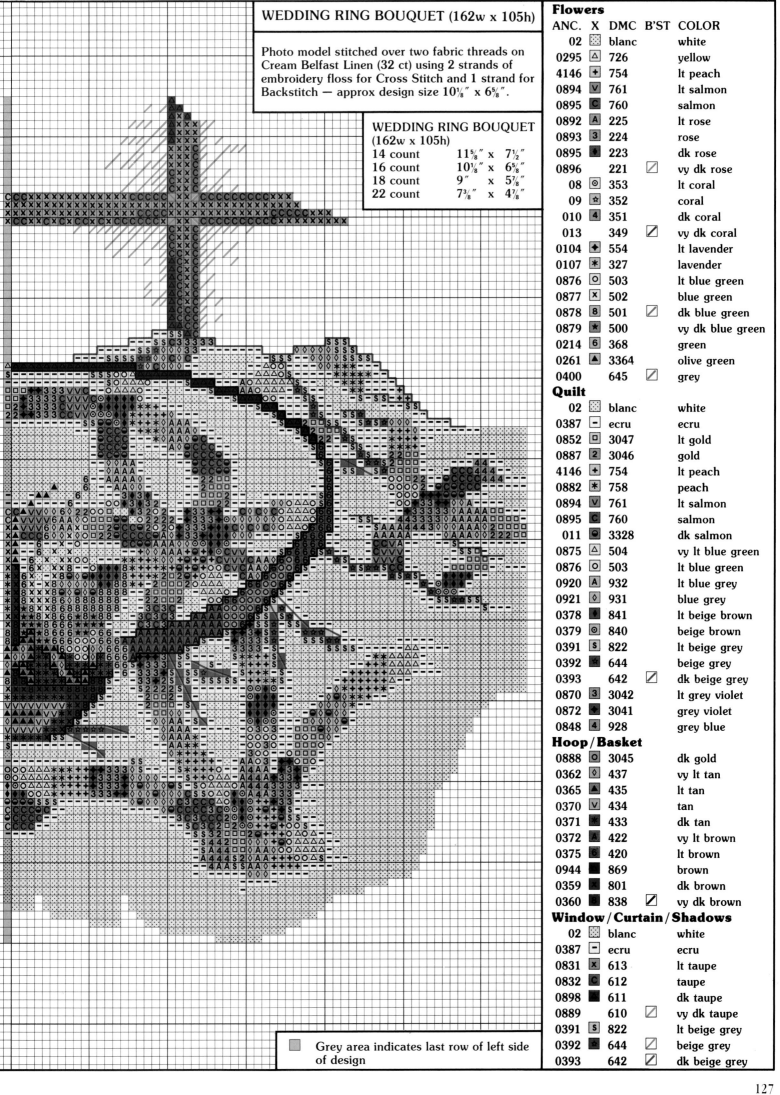

WEDDING RING BOUQUET (162w x 105h)

Photo model stitched over two fabric threads on Cream Belfast Linen (32 ct) using 2 strands of embroidery floss for Cross Stitch and 1 strand for Backstitch — approx design size 10⅛″ x 6⅝″.

WEDDING RING BOUQUET (162w x 105h)

14 count	11⅝″	x 7½″
16 count	10⅛″	x 6⅝″
18 count	9″	x 5⅞″
22 count	7⅜″	x 4⅞″

Flowers

ANC.	X	DMC	B'ST	COLOR
02	▨	blanc		white
0295	△	726		yellow
4146	✚	754		lt peach
0894	V	761		lt salmon
0895	C	760		salmon
0892	A	225		lt rose
0893	3	224		rose
0895	✦	223		dk rose
0896		221	╱	vy dk rose
08	⊙	353		lt coral
09	☆	352		coral
010	4	351		dk coral
013		349	╱	vy dk coral
0104	✦	554		lt lavender
0107	✳	327		lavender
0876	⊙	503		lt blue green
0877	X	502		blue green
0878	8	501	╱	dk blue green
0879	★	500		vy dk blue green
0214	6	368		green
0261	▲	3364		olive green
0400		645	╱	grey

Quilt

ANC.	X	DMC	B'ST	COLOR
02	▨	blanc		white
0387	-	ecru		ecru
0852	▣	3047		lt gold
0887	2	3046		gold
4146	✚	754		lt peach
0882	✳	758		peach
0894	V	761		lt salmon
0895	C	760		salmon
011	▣	3328		dk salmon
0875	△	504		vy lt blue green
0876	⊙	503		lt blue green
0920	A	932		lt blue grey
0921	◇	931		blue grey
0378	◈	841		lt beige brown
0379	⊙	840		beige brown
0391	S	822		lt beige grey
0392	✦	644		beige grey
0393		642	╱	dk beige grey
0870	3	3042		lt grey violet
0872	✦	3041		grey violet
0848	4	928		grey blue

Hoop / Basket

ANC.	X	DMC	B'ST	COLOR
0888	⊙	3045		dk gold
0362	◇	437		vy lt tan
0365	▲	435		lt tan
0370	V	434		tan
0371	✳	433		dk tan
0372	A	422		vy lt brown
0375	6	420		lt brown
0944	■	869		brown
0359	✕	801		dk brown
0360	▨	838	╱	vy dk brown

Window / Curtain / Shadows

ANC.	X	DMC	B'ST	COLOR
02	▨	blanc		white
0387	-	ecru		ecru
0831	✕	613		lt taupe
0832	C	612		taupe
0898	■	611		dk taupe
0889		610	╱	vy dk taupe
0391	S	822		lt beige grey
0392	✦	644	╱	beige grey
0393		642	╱	dk beige grey

■ Grey area indicates last row of left side of design

127

GENERAL INSTRUCTIONS
WORKING WITH CHARTS

How To Read Charts: Each of the designs is shown in chart form. Each colored square on the charts represents one Cross Stitch or one Half Cross Stitch. Each colored triangle on the charts represents one Quarter Stitch. Colored dots represent French Knots. Colored ovals represent Lazy Daisy Stitches. The straight lines on the charts indicate Backstitch. When a French Knot, Lazy Daisy Stitch, or Backstitch covers a square, the symbol is omitted.

Each chart is accompanied by a color key. This key indicates the color of floss to use for each stitch on the chart. The headings on the color key are for Cross Stitch (**X**), DMC color number (**DMC**), Quarter Stitch (**¹/₄X**), Half Cross Stitch (**¹/₂X**), Backstitch (**B'ST**), Anchor color number (**ANC.**) or J. & P. Coats color number (**JPC**), and color name (**COLOR**). Color key columns should be read vertically and horizontally to determine type of stitch and floss color.

STITCHING TIP

Working Over Two Fabric Threads: Use the sewing method instead of the stab method when working over two fabric threads. To use the sewing method, keep your stitching hand on the right side of the fabric (instead of stabbing the fabric with the needle and taking your stitching hand to the back of the fabric to pick up the needle). With the sewing method, you take the needle down and up with one stroke instead of two. To add support to stitches, it is important that the first Cross Stitch is placed on the fabric with stitch 1-2 beginning and ending where a vertical fabric thread crosses over a horizontal fabric thread *(Fig. 1)*. When the first stitch is in the correct position, the entire design will be placed properly, with vertical fabric threads supporting each stitch.

Fig. 1

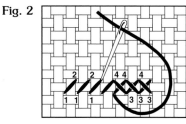

STITCH DIAGRAMS

Counted Cross Stitch (X): Work one Cross Stitch to correspond to each colored square on the chart. For horizontal rows, work stitches in two journeys *(Fig. 2)*. For vertical rows, complete each stitch as shown *(Fig. 3)*. When working over two fabric threads, work Cross Stitch as shown in **Fig. 4**. When the chart shows a Backstitch crossing a colored square *(Fig. 5)*, a Cross Stitch *(Fig. 2, 3, or 4)* should be worked first; then the Backstitch *(Fig. 10 or 11)* should be worked on top of the Cross Stitch.

Fig. 2

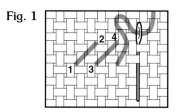

Fig. 3

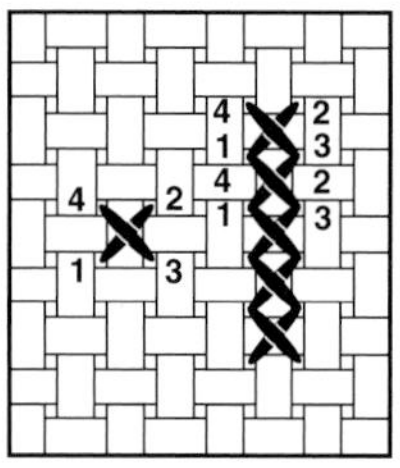

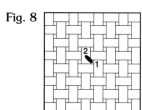

Fig. 4

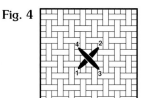

Fig. 5

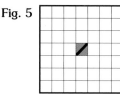

Half Cross Stitch (¹/₂X): This stitch is one journey of the Cross Stitch and is worked from lower left to upper right as shown in **Fig. 6**. When working over two fabric threads, work Half Cross Stitch as shown in **Fig. 7**.

Fig. 6

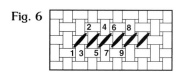

Fig. 7

Quarter Stitch (¹/₄X): Quarter Stitches are denoted by triangular shapes of color on the chart and on the color key. Come up at 1 *(Fig. 8)*; then split fabric thread to go down at 2. **Fig. 9** shows the technique for Quarter Stitch when working over two fabric threads.

Fig. 8

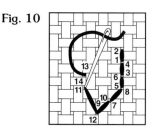

Fig. 9

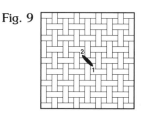

Backstitch (B'ST): For outline detail, Backstitch (shown on chart and on color key by colored straight lines) should be worked after the design has been completed *(Fig. 10)*. When working over two fabric threads, work Backstitch as shown in **Fig. 11**.

Fig. 10

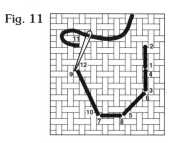

Fig. 11

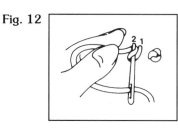

French Knot: Bring needle up at 1. Wrap floss once around needle and insert needle at 2, holding end of floss with non-stitching fingers *(Fig. 12)*. Tighten knot; then pull needle through fabric, holding floss until it must be released. For larger knot, use more strands; wrap only once.

Fig. 12

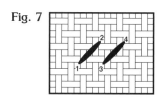

Lazy Daisy Stitch: Bring needle up at 1 and make a loop. Go down at 1 and come up at 2, keeping floss below point of needle *(Fig. 13)*. Pull needle through and go down at 2 to anchor loop, completing stitch. *(**Note:** To support stitches, it may be helpful to go down in edge of next fabric thread when anchoring loop.)*

Fig. 13

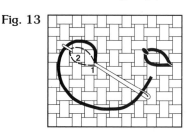

We have made every effort to ensure that these instructions are accurate and complete. We cannot, however, be responsible for human error, typographical mistakes, or variations in individual work.